D1603295

Revealing Antiquity

· 1 ·

G. W. Bowersock, General Editor

Dionysos at Large

Marcel Detienne

TRANSLATED BY
Arthur Goldhammer

HARVARD UNIVERSITY PRESS
Cambridge, Massachusetts
London, England
1989

Copyright © 1989 by the President and Fellows of
Harvard College
All rights reserved
Printed in the United States of America
10 9 8 7 6 5 4 3 2 1

Originally published as *Dionysos à ciel ouvert,* © Hachette, 1986,
in the series *Textes du XXᵉ siècle,* under the direction of Maurice
Olender.

Library of Congress Cataloging-in-Publication Data

Detienne, Marcel.
[Dionysos à ciel ouvert. English]
Dionysos at large / Marcel Detienne : translated by Arthur
Goldhammer.   p. cm.—(Revealing antiquity)
Translation of: Dionysos à ciel ouvert.
Includes index.
ISBN 0-674-20773-4 (alk. paper)
1. Dionysus (Greek deity)   I. Title.   II. Series.
BL820.B2D4513 1989   88-21474
292'.211—dc19   CIP

CONTENTS

Prolegomena

  BACCHUS is a living god, while Dionysos today smacks of the scholarly. With every libation poured the world over, Bacchus' youth is restored, and the more sophisticated the culture of wine, the more intense is the presence of what Baudelaire called "the mysterious god hidden in the fibers of the vine." Without any doubt, Dionysos is the most cosmopolitan of the Greek gods. According to the ambassador of King Seleucus, who, after Alexander, discovered India and its divinities, only Dionysos could match Siva—the Benevolent as much as the Terrible—who reaps death in every victim sacrificed. And when the Gentiles, contemporaries of Plutarch, evoked the god of Israel, he of the harvest and the gathering of fruits, it was again Dionysos—already Osiris of Egypt—who was named.

Of the gods that can be encountered throughout Greece, Dionysos is the least sedentary. Nowhere is he at home. Certainly not in Thebes, where his mother, the mortal Semele, carried him for several months in her belly. He is a nomadic god; his kingdom knows no capital. Never is he more constricted than when he wears the mask of the god, shrouded in incense and decorated with medals. Athens' rather starchy Dionysos thoroughly deceived his worshipers—there is no question about his powers of illusion, however sumptuous his thrones and official rostrums. Dionysos must be left to his provinces, his villages, his roving ways. He must be granted the full freedom of his epiphanies. Let him show himself in Anatolia, on the outskirts of Sardis, on the slopes of Tmolos raising a goblet of excellent wine—tmolos, obviously—and mixing it with a little water to give to the goddess Rhea, his mother in these parts. Or let a noble vintage slosh over the rim of the barrel on the heights of Vesuvius as the Satyrs lead the dance, while Dionysos, his body shaped like a bunch of grapes tightly trussed in a gleaming gown of swollen seed, carelessly pours his panther a libation in undiluted gulps.

In Argos, Lesbos, Eleutherai, Olympia, Thasos, Delphi, and Orchomenos, on a mysterious island off the Atlantic coast, and in many other places, Dionysos surges, leaps, dances, grabs, rends, sows madness. The rainbow of his apparitions contains the kindred colors of spurting blood and frothing wine. Dionysos is the god who snatches his victim by surprise, who trips his prey and drags it down into madness, murder, and defilement; yet he is also the god of vines that ripen in a day, of fountains of wine, of the drink that intoxicates, that creates effervescence. Might this double god turn out to be one?

1. Epidemic, This God

℞ PROITOS, king of the Argolid, had three daughters. As they grew up they went mad, refusing to honor Dionysos. Abandoning their father's palace, they wandered throughout the kingdom. Proitos called upon Melampous, a soothsayer and renowned purifier, whose incantations and medicinal herbs pacified and purified the women. For his trouble Melampous demanded a third of the kingdom. When the king refused, the malady grew worse. His daughters became increasingly agitated, and madness overtook the rest of the female population. Women left their homes, disappeared into the woods, killed their children. Eventually Melampous received two-thirds of the kingdom.[1]

In this story the madness, or *mania,* spread by Dionysos takes the form of a malady that attacks a great number of people. The three daughters are the first to succumb, but before long not a woman in the realm is spared.[2] In this and other, similar tales, "dionysism" takes on epidemic proportions.[3] (An epidemic like this one required no theory of contagion, of which Greek medicine had no notion before the historian Thucydides undertook to describe the plague in Athens.)[4] Reading the story of the Proitides, Erwin Rohde imagined the spread of dionysism in terms of an epidemic of convulsive dancing, a contagious disease like Saint Vitus' dance.[5] To be sure, Dionysiac madness was as contagious as spilt blood was defiling. In Greek, however, the word "epidemic" belonged to the vocabulary of theophany. Emile Littré, the nineteenth-century French lexicographer, was aware of this when he introduced the word into the French language.[6] It was a technical term used in talking about the gods. "Epidemics" were sacrifices offered to the divine powers when they came to visit a region or a temple or attended a feast or were present at a sacrifice.[7] Symmetrically, "apodemics" were sacrifices offered upon the gods' departure. For there was a traffic of the gods, a traffic that became particularly heavy during Theoxenia, occasions when a city, individual, or god offered hospitality to some or all of the deities.[8] The gods came to the place and lived there for a time; they were actually present,[9] or "epidemized." Being resident but not sedentary, they resembled the Hippocratic physicians, itinerant practitioners who composed what were called Epidemics: sheafs of notes, brief protocols or, rather, minutes relating the course of the disease—a careful record of the symptoms, the crisis, the care administered, and the patient's reactions.[10] The technique was that of a reporter, practiced by Ion of Chios, an intellectual of the fifth century B.C., in his work entitled *Epidemics:* a series of sketches, portraits, interviews with artists like Sophocles and politicians like Pericles and Kimon of Athens.[11]

The deities who were greeted with "epidemics" were the migrant gods: the Dioskouroi, Artemis, Apollo. They had their seasons. People invoked them; they sang

hymns inviting them to come. Apollo, for one, traveled
frequently from temple to temple, from Delos to Miletus
to Delphi and the Hyperborean regions where he liked to
winter. He was a god of epiphanies, with his feast days and
his anniversaries. He appeared among his priests, amid
crowds of believers, in all the splendor of his might. But
apart from Apollo the most epidemic of the gods of the
pantheon was surely Dionysos,[12] whose presence (*parousia*) was a prime means of action.[13] Dionysos was in
essence the god who comes: he appears, he manifests
himself,[14] he makes his presence known. He was an
itinerant epiphany; all geography was arranged to suit his
mobile activities. Present everywhere, he had no home,[15]
no mountain lair or redoubt or sanctuary entrance or
well-lighted urban temple. His effigy fell from heaven
above, his ship loomed on the sea's horizon. At the head of
a female commando he stormed city gates or, alone,
emerged from the watery abyss at Lerna in Argolis. In
Dionysos there was an "epidemic" drive, which set him
apart from other gods with regular, programmed epiphanies, always amenable to the official order of feasts and
each with his or her fixed time. Neither the faithful nor the
gods were surprised by their arrivals. On the seventh day
of the month of Bysios, Apollo, founder of the oracle,
invariably arrived at the temple at Delphi. Dionysos, in
contrast, always on the move and perpetually changing
form, was never sure of being recognized as he went from
town to village wearing the mask of a strange power,
unlike any other. There was always the chance, moreover,
that he would be denied membership in the race of gods.[16]
Roving was too much his natural condition to permit his
arrivals, his comings and goings, to be confused with
those of the other gods.

Epidemic, This God

A Unique Mask

6   Dionysos was epidemic (in the strong sense of the word) in a series of stories, more terrifying than joyful, that were told more or less everywhere whenever he arrived. His first epiphanies were marked by confrontation, conflict, or hostility, in forms ranging from misrecognition and disavowal to outright rejection and even persecution. In these stories, in which a god is not only greeted with hostility but accused of being a foreigner, how can we fail to hear something like an echo, frozen in memory, of a concrete and very real history? The script has been continually rewritten by the moderns. Some hold that the stranger from the north was the God of Thrace and Phrygia, who carried with him the virus of the trance and a savage religiosity;[17] others, that he was a southern god returning home to the Peloponnese after a long absence occasioned by the Doric and aristocratic invasion.[18]

The imagined routes of Dionysos' travels were a subject of ancient tradition, embodied in myth or tragedy. In the *Bacchae,* for instance, the Lydian chorus evokes the three rivers crossed along the route from the forests of the Pangaeus to Pieria.[19] Yet there is no good reason to think that a god so quick to appear and disappear would have left unambiguous traces of his journeys through a country in which he always claimed to be a stranger, even when he came to the city of Thebes where he was supposed to have been born (or even twice born).

Why should Dionysiac mythology repeatedly dwell on the god's epiphany and its beginnings among the peoples and cities of Greece unless the stories were somehow revealing of the essence of his divine nature? In examining accounts of the Dionysian parousia, I shall attempt to pinpoint what it was in these continual appearances that distinguished this god's mode of action from that of all others.

If one were to classify the stories of Dionysos, the god who comes, they would, I think, fall readily into three categories. First, there are those in which the god's arrival is indirect: he has ambassadors who introduce his cult, bring his effigy, or erect his idol. At Elis where he serenely shares a table with his stepmother, Hera, his cult is supposed to have been founded by a couple of natives, a mother and son.[20] At Sikyon, a Theban by the name of Phanes the Apparitor acts as ambassador, bringing from his native city a statue of Dionysos Lysios, highly recommended by the Delphic oracle.[21] Finally, Dionysos comes to Patras in unusual company, that of a more or less mad king, who carries in his coffer a terrifying statue of the god.[22] These brief stories, few in number, have little to tell us about Dionysos himself or his manifestations.[23]

A second type of epidemic involves the god of the vine, the wine god and his host. Dionysos comes and leaves behind not only the secret of vinegrowing but the promise of a fermented drink, which carries with it a madness to be tempered, a savage power to be tamed. Athenian tradition gives us a refined epiphany of the god of the intoxicating cup, making visible the mediations that ultimately resulted in the etiquette of the symposium. We also see the dark underside: the spontaneous resurgence of a god whose manifestations are sudden and brutal. From these the richest Dionysian tales would be constructed.

The third series of Dionysian stories includes the arrival at the home of Lykourgos, the apparition in the palace of the Minyades, and the great parousia in the city of Thebes. These three epiphanies reveal the nature of

Dionysos' power in decisive fashion. They offer three examples of confirmed madness, of *mania* leading to murder and defilement—a journey to the end of the night in the frenzied wake of Dionysos.

By his epiphanic virtues the god who comes knows intimately the affinities of presence and absence. Whether he walks in smiles or leaps in irritation, Dionysos always appears in the guise of the stranger. He is the god who comes from outside, who arrives from Elsewhere. One story from Lesbos is particularly revealing. It is told by Pausanias in the course of his visit to the temple at Delphi.[24] The Periegete has just made a tour of the temple and noted the ex-votos on the terrace, and he is preparing to describe the pediments on which Apollo and the Muses respond to Dionysos flanked by the Thyiades. Perhaps he had noticed a small temple of Dionysos Sphaleotas, the god "who causes stumbling."[25]

> A fishermen's net at Methymne drew up from the sea a face (*prosopon*) made of olive wood: it had a look about it that was definitely godlike, but foreign, and not in the tradition of Greek gods. So the Methymnians asked the Pythian priestess what god or maybe divine hero it was a portrait of: she commanded them to worship Dionysos Sphalen.[26] The Methymnians keep the wooden head (*xoanon*) from the sea for themselves and honor it with prayers and sacrifices, but they sent a bronze one to Delphi.

A mask rises from the depths of the sea; an unknown face appears in the midst of a marine space that is like another world. But it is not a frightening face, like the Trojan idol of Dionysos, which drove mad anyone who

8

found it. It is rather an enigmatic form, an effigy to be deciphered, an unknown power to be identified. There is something divine in it, but it is a divinity other than that shared by the Hellenic gods—other in the sense that it is both strange and foreign, reflecting the double meaning of the Greek word *xenos*. "Foreign" here refers not to the non-Greek, the barbarian who speaks an unintelligible tongue, but to the citizen of a neighboring community.[27] The *xenos* is produced by the distance that separates two cities: in their sacrifices, their assemblies, and their tribunals. In order to be called *xenos,* a stranger therefore had to come from the Hellenic world, ideally consisting of those who shared "one blood, one language, and common sanctuaries and sacrifices."[28] When Dionysos appears to Pentheus the Theban, he is wearing the mask of the foreigner. It is to a *xenos* that the king of Thebes speaks.[29] Despite his Lydian disguise, Dionysos is treated as a Greek.

Since the discovery of Mycenaean, we no longer have any doubt that Dionysos is Greek; but the Greeks never did. Nowhere was Dionysos ever characterized as a barbarian god, not even when his violence seemed to exile him once and for all into the barbarous world. In this respect he stands in sharp contrast with another deity who in other ways resembles him: Artemis, who is called Orthia and whose statue causes madness and sets worshipers to killing one another over her altar. Some claim that this Artemis is of Tauric origin, that she is a *barbarous* deity,[30] compared with which Dionysos exhibits his nature as a foreign god, a *xenos,* when he makes his joyous entry into Pátras in Achaia, where a bloody Artemis reigns. He does this in a most unusual way. Dionysos is introduced as a foreign demon, a *xenikos daimon,* an idol carried in a

9

trunk by an equally foreign king. Indeed, the king is doubly *xenos*, because one day in Troy he lost his mind, it was said, while contemplating the mask of the god who from that moment on possessed him and guided his travels.[31] As foretold by the Delphic oracle, the king and his odd entourage came to cleanse Patras of the stain of human blood periodically spilled on the orders of a resentful Artemis.

The Strange Stranger

Dionysos' personality is deeply colored by his status as stranger. He encourages a personal, individual relationship with those who worship him, and invariably in revealing himself he wears a mask. When the gods march in procession along a frieze, Dionysos' mask is the sign of his divinity. He puts on his face as spontaneously as Hermes carries the caduceus. The François vase gives prominence to his wide-open eyes, which fix on the spectator who contemplates the parade of Olympians. By way of the mask that confers upon him his figurative identity, Dionysos affirms his epiphanic nature as a god who continually alternates between presence and absence.[32] He is always a stranger, a form to identify, a face to uncover, a mask that hides as much as it reveals. But coming as a *xenos* into the territory of another city, Dionysos demands to be treated socially as any stranger would be treated in Greece: he is received as a private guest, whether by a peasant or by a king. A private citizen, an ordinary individual takes it upon himself to receive and protect a stranger on his travels. The *proxenos* was a local citizen who looked after foreign interests in a Greek city-state.[33] Perhaps it was because Dionysos, the traveling god, was associated with this institution that he chose a companion by the name of Proxenos. He is mentioned at Delphi in connection with the temple of Apollo, where the *proxenes* of so many cities jostled one another. Foreigners who came to consult the oracle or to participate in panhellenic festivals did not have the right to make sacrifices in the temple without the mediation of their patrons.[34]

On the relief published in 1936, the Proxenos of the Dionysian cortege[35] raises a rhyton, a Dionysian drinking vessel, and pours its contents into a cinnamon-colored phial, a familiar accoutrement of the cult of Apollo. Half-lying on an inclined plane, he strikes the same pose as the Pan with cantharus in the cave of Thasos. But this Delphian Proxenos of Dionysos is entirely naked and has a snub nose, thick lips, and two pointy ears.[36] He is thus a satyr serving as *proxenos* for his master, who for once appears to be wearing the mask of a god in his home, at variance with his character of perpetual wanderer and stranger. But it is the divinity who comes from outside the city that makes the individual relationship important: Dionysos is received by a host, hence he is a god of election. Around him as the trance progressed formed the thiasos, a small group subject to no dominion other than its own, which organized to serve Bacchus.[37] If our most vivid image of Dionysos is now preeminently as god of the thiasos, the group in which religious life became an individual affair, we must remember that the path of his travels was determined by his foreign status.

Let us return now to the other meaning of *xenos,* evoked by the olive-wood mask dredged up by the Methymnian fishermen in their nets. There is something peculiar and strange about the face that emerges from the sea. In Pausanias' account *xenos* occurs in the position of an adjective,[38] the meaning of which is given by the paraphrase: "which did not fit any of the Greek gods." The material of which the mask is made—the wood of the olive tree rather than the contorted stock of the vine[39]—already suggests a tranquil epiphany, which makes it possible to detail the mask's unusual appearance, rather than, as often happens, being struck or even assaulted by the strangeness of the unknown face. Here the strangeness points toward the oracle; it elicits questions about the nature of the idol that has been dredged up. These questions are asked without anxiety or reticence, with a serenity not always evident when Dionysos appears. For if Semele's son were simply a *xenos*, a foreigner eager to undergo metamorphosis into a guest through the immediate generosity of festivals for *xenia* or of *xenismos*,[40] the banquets sometimes staged by the cities he visited, he could have come like other guests of divine rank to regularly scheduled Theoxenia, where his visits could have been celebrated in pure joy.[41]

In his most memorable epiphanies, Dionysos is equally strange and a stranger. He is the Stranger who brings strangeness. But it is a strangeness occasioned by misrecognition or, rather, nonrecognition. Pausanias' tale gives the obvious reason for this: a foreign god is an unknown, so much so that the Methymnians cannot decide whether he is a god or a hero. How does one recognize a god whom one does not know? What is more, Dionysos' divinity is of recent date.[42] Had he not, as Herodotus points out, been born to Semele, daughter of Kadmos, barely a thousand years earlier?[43] And there is a persistent rumor, noted by Dionysos himself when he appears in Thebes at the beginning of the *Bacchae*, that he is Semele's natural child and not the son of Zeus by a mortal woman.[44] Despite this slander, Dionysos, like Herakles, is treated as an official bastard of Zeus, and he begins his career as a poor relation of the Olympian clan. Dionysos needs to win recognition of himself as a divine power, at least in the world of men.[45] This is his obsession in the Theban parousia, the most elaborate of his epiphanies. In Boeotia as well as Argolis Dionysos is a god who experiences the humiliation of being treated as a mere mortal or even an impostor.[46] He is unrecognized by some and mistaken by others. The incredulous refuse to believe in him, while the foolish consider him unimportant and the hostile refuse to listen to discussions of his rites. Worse still, there are those whose vocation it is to persecute him, to assume the role of torturers; when they become victims themselves, they stand as striking witnesses to his parousia as an omnipotent god.

First in the series of villains is Lykourgos, king of the Edonians. For it was in Thrace, presumed to be the place outside Greece from which Dionysos hailed, that he encountered his first adversary. The Homeric Lykourgos appears in the *Iliad* as the enemy of the gods, "seeking a dispute with the Uranian deities."[47] He is a professional of impiety, indeed a raging brute who attacks Dionysos on the sacred Nyseon, a murderer (*androphonos*)[48] who hurls himself on the nurses of the raging Dionysos (Mainomenos), disperses the thyrsus bearers, and pursues the frightened young god. This story was rewritten by Aeschylus in the *Edoni*:[49] the Bacchae are in chains, the troop of Satyrs are imprisoned, but this time Dionysos draws Lykourgos to the limits of his madness and turns the possessed man's desire for violence and murder back against him. The chains of the maenads who carry the thyrsi fall away of their own accord. The high walls of the

Epidemic, This God

royal palace begin to totter, and the roof begins to dance as if in a bacchic delirium. Lykourgos, too, falls mad.[50] Raising his two-headed hatchet, he tries to strike at the accursed vine that the Stranger has brought. But Dionysos, clouding his vision, directs him toward his son, the terrified vine-child, who tries to escape. The raging king cuts the shoots and slices through the stalk of the vine. Dionysos waits until Lykourgos has cut off his child's limbs, then restores his reason. Having become the murderer of his son, Lykourgos turns all the land sterile for miles around. On advice of the Delphic oracle, the Edonians transport him, bound, to the frozen forests of Mount Pangaeus, where, as Herodotus had seen,[51] there is a temple of a Dionysian oracle. The oracle speaks through the mouth of a woman, who, like Apollo on the heights of Delphi, is surrounded by her priests. Left to die in territory over which Dionysos seems to have reigned in solitary sovereignty, the guilty king is torn apart by wild horses.

Madness and Defilement for Entire Generations

From Argos to Orchomenos Dionysos traveled by the same routes to the Theban epiphany, culmination of the dark madness. The scenario is the same. Dionysos is denied his rites. Frenzied women begin to wander about the countryside, already suffering from a disease that requires a physician, a defilement that calls for purification. The madness grows worse, affecting all women, who, though driven into the brush, return to murder their children. Thus there are two degrees of madness, the second resulting in the utmost defilement, the spilling of a son's blood by his own mother.

It is in Boeotia, however, in Thebes and Orchomenos, that the Dionysiac parousia produces its most extreme effects. First to be touched are the Minyades, the three daughters of King Orchomenos.[52] They criticize the other women, who desert the city for the mountains, where they become bacchae. Dionysos offers them a chance to recognize his divine nature. Disguised as a young girl, he exhorts the Minyades not to neglect the god's rites and mysteries, but they pay no attention, provoking Dionysos' wrath. He appears to them in the form of a bull, a lion, and a leopard. Meanwhile, the loom, a tool that symbolizes the Minyades' domestic vocation, begins to exude milk and nectar from its uprights. Frightened by these prodigies, the three sisters hasten to join the cult of Dionysos and participate with abandon in the ceremonies of the new god. "Without wasting a moment, all three put lots into a vessel and shook it. Out fell that of Leukippe, who vowed to offer a victim to Dionysos, and with the help of her sisters she rent the flesh of her own son."[53]

Two of the three known versions of this story[54] tell us about the aftermath of the frenzy that turned the Minyades into murderesses. In Aelian's account they dance away in the direction of Kithairon, where they participate in the mountain revels that precede the dismemberment of a son by his mother. Once Dionysos has been given his due, they bound off, merry and joyful, to meet the other maenads. But the latter reject them straightaway, drive them away, and hasten after them "on account of their defilement (agos)." The well-behaved bacchae of Orchomenos do not identify with the murderous folly of Minyas' daughters. But it is only in Plutarch's version that the full consequences of the taint become apparent, establishing the basis for a Dionysiac ritual that was still practiced in

Boeotia in the first century A.D. There, according to Plutarch, the three Minyades are described as having been mad from the outset. By the grace of Dionysos they are gripped with a desire for human flesh. By lot they decide which of their children will satisfy that desire, and the mother designated by chance enjoys the honor of offering the god her own flesh, expertly dismembered. This sacrificial murder, given added zest by the desire to devour the victim, makes the Minyades resemble the Bassarai, those fanatics of human sacrifice on the altars of Dionysos who pursued horror to its logical conclusion by devouring one another.[55]

From that day on in Orchomenos the husbands of the Minyades, in mourning, were known as Psoloeis, meaning "with face darkened by smoke," and the Minyades themselves were given the epithet Oleiai, which Plutarch paraphrases as "fatal, pernicious." In the time of Plutarch the descendants of the *genos* of the Minyades were assigned this title. Every two years, during the feast of Agrionia,[56] the people of Orchomenos honored Dionysos by replaying the scene of exile and pursuit. The women of the murderous clan were again hunted down, as the Minyades had been after defiling themselves by spilling their own blood. The chase was led not by the bacchae, however, but by the priest of Dionysos, sword in hand: "He is permitted to kill any woman whom he catches in the chase." It is as if the descendants of the Minyades continued to bear a mark of opprobrium that made it legitimate for any citizen of Orchomenos (represented in the ritual by the priest of Dionysos) to strike them down. To be sure, this is now an official Dionysos. But after many generations he is still capable of manifesting his resentment against those who recognized him too late.

Epidemic, This God

In Orchomenos there was a strict division between the daughters of Minyas and other women. "Many are the thyrsus-bearers, few are the Bacchoi," was the expression used by "those who deal with initiations," the disciples of Orpheus and experts in *teletai,* who gave such prominence to Dionysos.[57] Here the god proceeded in the same way as in Thebes. Leading the way were the docile women, the gray flock of wives who set out on the path to Kithairon. Their tranquil madness became the pretext for the true epiphany, the experience of the Minyades, who revealed the radical strangeness of the god of *mania.* Their possession made them strangers to themselves, murderesses whose defilement cut them off from the rest of the community.

In Thebes between Kadmos and Agave, impurity and exile were written even more vividly in letters of blood. Thebes, having witnessed the birth of Dionysos, was serenely free to mistake his identity. In his native territory even more than in Orchomenos, Dionysos wore the mask of the Stranger. The Theban royal family, blind to the evidence of his divine nature, "will know that it is not initiated into the service of Bacchus."[58] Hearing "his relatives deny that he was a god,"[59] Dionysos determined to show them the cost of tardiness in recognizing who he was. The murder of Pentheus, the defilement of Agave, the exile of Kadmos were all striking and flagrant examples of violence that revealed in unforgettable fashion the nature of Dionysos' divinity. The Dionysiac parousia attains its height when Strangeness turns up in its native soil. In what theater does the action unfold? Behind the stage occupied by the god who comes as *xenos* lies another stage, evoked by his dual birth in the thunder-riven womb of his mother, Semele.

Epidemic, This God

Dionysos' Theban epiphany was played out between two sanctuaries intimately associated with each other in the religious and cult history of Kadmos' country. One was the tomb of Semele, the bridal chamber of a woman delivered of her child by heaven's fire, a charred, forbidden place where a mother lay awaiting the coming of her son and avenger. With his first words Dionysos indicates the location of the tomb.[60] But he pretends to ignore what spectators familiar with Thebes and its gods knew and saw: "against Semele's wall" another sanctuary, that of Dionysos Kadmeios.[61] In other words, it is the temple of a great god of Thebes, the very one evoked by the chorus in *Oedipus Rex:* after Apollo the Lycian, the savior, the god with bow, here is Bacchus with his cry of "evoe," wearing a crimson mask, companion of the wandering Maenads and eponymous god of Thebes, who takes his name from Kadmos the autochthonous.[62] Attested by inscriptions from the third century B.C., Dionysos Kadmeios reigned alongside Apollo over the assembly of Theban gods.[63] And the feast celebrated in his honor every two years bore the same name as the Orchomenian ritual involving the Minyades: Agrionia. Hence the god who presented himself to the city as a stranger was of all the gods of Thebes the most powerful next to Apollo, who is here again his accomplice.[64] This would be paradoxical if Dionysos were really as foreign a god as the Thracian Bendis or the Syrian Adonis. If, however, Strangeness is a structural component of Dionysos' divinity, it is not surprising that strangeness should manifest itself most forcefully in the region and city where he was most at home. The closer the relation between Dionysos and those who mistake his identity, the more urgent is his need to be recognized and the more violent his epiphany. In the region of Thebes, among his own people, Dionysos can no longer hide that he is the Stranger within or that the strangeness of his parousia is essential to his nature as a god without synonym.

In the Agrionia Dionysos entices the daughters of Kadmos into the same murderous madness as the daughters of Minyas. For love of Semele he himself chooses the child who will be torn apart and sacrificed by its mother before her eyes. Pentheus dismembered by Agave is the tragic inversion of the Dionysian couple, so present in Thebes, of the son and mother locked in amorous embrace. Compared with the frenzy of Agave and her thiasos, the chorus of Lydian bacchae in Euripides' play occupies the same place as the women of Orchomenos who peacefully cavort as maenads on Kithairon. In the Theban tragedy Dionysos himself states what punishment he has reserved for Kadmos and Agave.[65] Like the impure Minyades who are driven from the land, the mother of Pentheus is forced into exile. She is banished from her father's home, wrenched from her fatherland.[66] Dionysos explains why: "You are obliged, as a murderess, to leave the city."[67] Agave's regrets echo this judgment: "Had I not spread on my hands a stain (*musos*) of this kind."[68] Elsewhere Dionysos heaps abuse upon Agave and her sisters: "They must leave their city in order to expiate the sacrilegious defilement (*anosion miasma*) with regard to those whom they have massacred. They will never see their fatherland again, for piety will not permit murderers to live among their victims' graves."[69] The fate of Kadmos' daughters is that reserved for homicides: on grounds of impurity they are banished from Thebes.

In Orchomenos Dionysos condemned the descendants of the Minyades to bear the taint of their ancestors.

In Thebes it was not the descendants but the forebears who were the target of his wrath, particularly Kadmos, grandfather of Pentheus. Showing no weakness toward the male sex, the god in foreign mask banished the founder of the line. Like his daughters, Kadmos had to leave his homeland and vanish among the Barbarians. What is more, Dionysos compelled the "sower of the Theban race"[70] to lead an army of barbarians against Greece. Crueler still, the god obliged Kadmos to behave in the manner of a barbarian conqueror, destroying the most sacred possessions of the Greeks, the altars of the gods and the ancestral tombs, until the founder of Thebes and his wife reached the gates of Delphi and "sack the temple of Loxias."[71] Kadmos was transformed into a serpent, and in order to be delivered from his monstrous form and settle in Harmony in the land of the Blessed he was obliged to descend to the uttermost depths of impurity and commit the highest sacrilege, sacking the panhellenic temple of Apollo and destroying the residence of the god who was the other great god of his abandoned Thebes.

Beneath Two Identical Effigies

Melampous' role in the traditions of Argos and Sikyon has been taken to indicate that *mania* was seen as both a disease and a defilement. Madness fell within the competence of the soothsayer, the magus, and the purifier, who employed rival or complementary techniques: incantations, medicinal herbs, corybantic dancing, or anointment with purifying blood. Because Dionysiac madness or *mania* unhinged its victims, separating them from themselves and others, it contained elements of impurity. From Lykourgos to Agave one form of defilement led inevitably to another:

the impurity engendered by murder, the unclean hands of the infanticide, incurred the further defilement of madness. There is considerable homology between the murderer and the lunatic: insanity impels the murderer to act, and he is often viewed as a man possessed. It is the purifying aspect of Dionysos that is accentuated in the violent parousias of Baccheios or Baccheus. The more insanity is unleashed, the more room there is for catharsis.

Dionysos—divine child born of a mortal mother and persecuted by his stepmother, Hera—is intimately familiar with both, as is attested by his biography. In Apollodorus' *Bibliotheca* Dionysos, metamorphosed into a goat by his forewarned father, barely escapes the bloody madness that engulfs the abode of Athamas and Ino.[72] In Nysa, where Hermes has hastily hidden him, the young Dionysos discovers the vine. Hera, following close behind, this time aims her fury, her consuming rage, directly at him. Dionysos becomes delirious. *Mania* grips him—he who will become the god who leads men to madness—at a moment when intoxicating drink is evoked by the vine but while Dionysos is still under the power of Hera, herself an expert in mad rage.

He begins to wander between Egypt and Syria. Proteus, king of the Egyptians, is the first to receive him. But Dionysos continues on his way and is carried off to Phrygia, to the home of Cybele. He is then welcomed by Rhea, Mother of the gods, here distinct from her Phrygian double, the Mother with her cortege of tambourines, flutes, and *orgia*.[73] In Alexandrian imagery Dionysos, pursued by Hera, takes refuge on the altar of Rhea, a protective grandmother who saves him from his stepmother.[74] Significantly, Rhea puts an end to her grandson's madness. She "purifies" him, delivers him from his *mania*. And as Dionysos recovers his wits he learns his own ceremonies, his *teletai*. He receives from Rhea's hands his Bacchant's costume, his *stole*, before leaving for Thrace. Purification delivers him from the state of impurity in which he had been left by his *mania* and through some ritual apparently qualifies him to be made acquainted with his own ceremonial. In this context the *stole* is not a garment for covering nakedness but an accoutrement of the believer in Dionysos, a costume required for participation in his ceremonies, which he obliges the men and women of Thebes to wear.[75] Dionysos, a hunter disguised as a dresser, with great care arranges a bacchic garb—thyrsus, ivy, long robe, fawn-skin above—over the limbs of Pentheus in the *Bacchae*.[76] Whoever accepts this woman's dress is already afflicted with a slight madness.[77] But it is also the god's attire. Trapped in ritual garb that he wears as a mask, Pentheus is transformed into a Bacchus, a believer with an impious heart and guilty, as Dionysos frankly informs him, of wanting to see what those who do not become Bacchoi are not permitted to see.[78]

The Dionysos purified and cloaked and/or masked by Rhea combines two important aspects of ancient dionysism. One, more explicitly mythological, reveals the impurity of madness, of *mania* and the defilement it inflicts and the deliverance it calls forth. The other, more directly related to figures of ritual, demonstrates that the experience of a believer in Dionysos involves the reciprocal vision of the Bacchant and his god. "He saw me, I saw him; he bestowed upon me his *orgia*": Pentheus, curious about the ceremonies, hears these words spoken of the *teletai* brought by the Stranger.[79] Celebrant and celebrated share a single garment, beneath which both are other, that is, both are bacchants, in a state that is a common denominator between the god and the man. Thus, by being initiated into his own mysteries after enduring the trial of *mania,* Dionysos becomes what he is. He matures and at the same time he is recognized by the Olympian world. But he is a Dionysos whose divine history incorporates the essential elements of the religious experience that he introduces into the world of men under the sign of Strangeness: madness-defilement and purification, followed by mask-disguise coupled with the vision of brutal "faciality."

Dionysos stricken with *mania* and driven mad by Hera: despite his aversion to disrespectful myths, Plato, in the midst of his elderly companions, gives him a warm welcome.[80] He even draws from him a lesson for his philosophy of education: Dionysos is to lead the chorus of the elderly—but not the retired. For in Plato the elderly attain political and religious maturity. In *Laws* Dionysos is shown wreaking vengeance for the *mania* he has suffered by inventing for the human race the *baccheiai,* or Bacchic ceremonies, as well as all manner of entranced dancers (*manike . . . choreia*). In the same spirit Dionysos is said to have made us a gift of wine, a drug (*pharmakon*) so precious that in the city of the Magnetes it is to be administered in its pure state to the elderly, to whom it will bring "initiation and recreation" (*telete* and *paidia*).[81] Here the model is more detailed than in the *Bibliotheca,* and there is no digression concerning the trials of Dionysos. Here, in place of the *mania* induced by Hera, we have Bacchic madness and unwatered wine, either of which has the power to initiate.

Purification takes place in trance, in keeping with the usual cult practice.[82] This is true not only in Thebes but also in Sikyon and Corinth. In *Antigone,* when the entire city is in the grip of disease, of *nosos,* of the pestilence brought by the unburied dead, the choir turns to Bacchus, the god not only of Thebes but also of the heights of Delphi and of the temple at Eleusis. "Come with healing step from Parnassos' slope or over the moaning sea."[83] This is Dionysos Katharsios, the god who purifies, or the god who releases (Lysios) as he is called in Thebes. Once again he is accompanied by his mother, Semele, but in a temple located near the gates of the city at the place known as the Gates of the Proitides.[84] This Dionysos is god of an urban territory, which he dominates from his position as Kadmeios: power of the "ceremonies that deliver and purify."[85] Lysios or Katharsios, the god of Thebes reigns as a Bacchant; his native city cannot forget his parousias.

In the city of Kadmos, Dionysos appears divided in two, as he is in Sikyon, exhibiting two faces, bearing two names that are spoken and invoked in each year's ceremonial. Sikyon is the ancient Aigialeia, site of more than one august purification: of the daughters of Proitos by Melampous, and of Apollo when madness overtakes him after the murder of Python. Here Dionysos possesses two abodes.[86] One is a temple located below the Acropolis, behind the theater, where a visible god of gold and ivory sits among his white marble Bacchantes, sovereign over women who are consecrated to him (*hierai*) and who go into trances for him. "But the Sikyonians have other statues, which they keep secret. Once a year, at night, they transport them in procession from what they call the 'adorning place' (*kosmeterion*) to the Dionysion. The procession takes place by torchlight, and hymns of the region are sung. Leading the way is the statue known as Baccheios, built by Andromadas, son of Phlias. It is followed by the statue named Lysios, which the Theban Phanes brought from Thebes as instructed by the Pythia."[87] By cover of darkness Dionysos divides in two, abandoning his marble thiasos and his entranced ladies. He abandons his official effigy, and to the sound of hymns and by the light of torches he goes off wearing his two nighttime masks. At the head of the procession he appears as a Bacchant, as the god of frenzy. Farther back, however, he takes the form of a purifying power, Lysios, god of deliverance brought from Thebes and carried by a disciple of his epiphany, the aptly named Phanes. Dionysos' twofold power is apparent in this analytic staging of *mania,* which can be purification within madness precisely because it is first of all knowledge of the impurity of frenzied violence, which calls for subsequent purification. Dionysos follows a path between the two powers, Hera and Rhea, and everything else conforms to this fundamental fact.

In Corinth Dionysos' duality is openly exhibited in the agora in the form of two perfectly identical statues.[88] These are *xoana,* wooden statues covered with gold except for the face, which is painted crimson. In appearance nothing distinguishes one from the other. Nevertheless, one is called Lysios, the other Baccheios. Only the names belie the identity that is maintained even in the choice of materials. Our informant, Pausanias, recorded the words of the Corinthian exegetes concerning Pentheus' insult to Dionysos: his spying on the Dionysiac rites from a treetop, his body torn apart, and, after the drama, the Pythian oracle ordering the inhabitants of Corinth to find the bloody treetop and to revere it as a god. Two effigies of masked Dionysos are carved from the same violent wood, affirming the identity of Lysios and Baccheios from

Epidemic, This God

Thebes to the Kithairon. No attempt was made to differentiate the two aspects of the divinity, as the Naxians did with their two masks of Dionysos, the one named Baccheus being carved in the wood of vinestocks, the other, known as the Mild, the Soothing, Meilichios, being fashioned from the trunk of a fig tree.[89] The Corinthians, more sophisticated, created two statues with one mask and made of the same wood. They are identical twins, to each of which a voice assigns a name and thereby establishes a connection with one or the other extreme form of a power thus perfectly masked.

2. Inventing Wine and Distant Parousias

ℜ THE MOMENT we turn our attention from Thebes to Attica, this type of epiphany seems to disappear. It is replaced by another series of apparitions, in which Dionysos' behavior changes along with the setting. To Thebes, a city that neglected him most chastely and lovingly, Semele's son passed the fawnskin. He made the city his maenad, invested it from within, and possessed it in the most intimate part of its being, causing it to dance and to leap so violently that its founders, unhinged, were expelled and transformed into barbarians.

The Dionysos who made his way through Attica appeared in a totally different guise. He was a discreet, patient god, a benevolent and generous power—the opposite of his Theban character. This other Dionysos, who appeared from time to time in the country of Euripides, is not neglected in the *Bacchae,* where he is mentioned twice but as a remote, possibly unreal deity.[1] Tiresias is his only prophet. To Pentheus, who is about to misuse him, the soothsayer states the theological truth about the god who revealed himself in Thebes: "Mankind . . . possesses two supreme blessings. First of these is the goddess Demeter, or Earth—whichever name you choose to call her by. It was she who gave to man his nourishment of grain. But after her there came the son of Semele, who matched her present by inventing liquid wine as his gift to man. For filled with that good gift, suffering mankind forgets its grief; from it comes sleep; with it oblivion of the troubles of the day. There is no other medicine for misery. And when we pour libations to the gods, we pour the god of wine himself, that through his intercession man may win the favor of heaven."[2] Tiresias, the hoary bacchant, belongs to Apollo, the other great god of Thebes, and alone among those close to Pentheus he incurs none of Dionysos' resentment. "Without offending Phoibos he honored Bromios, the Great God (Megas Theos)."[3]

The Night Visitor

The divinity evoked by the soothsayer in his Theban setting was the Dionysos familiar to the Athenians, the god of the vine and of wine as he was when he came, according to the mythographers, in the time of King Pandionis.[4] It was then that Demeter, bearing food in the form of grain, entered the abode of Celeos, king of Eleusis. Meanwhile Dionysos, guest of Ikarios, hid the first vine plant in the folds of his cloak. The two great civilizing deities came in peace—and, in the case of Dionysos, with remarkable caution. Though heading for the temples and brilliant feasts that consecrated his presence in the heart of Athens, Dionysos chose an itinerary full of detours and erudite mediations. These detours followed a pattern, leading from the periphery to the center, but with two distinct entry points: one in northeast Athens, in the deme of Ikarion, the other to the northwest in the village of Eleutherai close to the border of Theban territory. Dionysos also showed himself adept at mediated interventions, practicing a measured and deliberate "epidemic" in keeping with a well-conceived global strategy that led by way of the grand procession route to the religious center of the city of Athens.

29

This Dionysos was notable for his reserve. He scarcely allowed himself to be noticed, leaving it to Apollo's oracle to point out, when he came with Pegasos to the gates of Athens, that "Dionysos had previously made the journey in the time of Ikarios."[5] But that time his appearance had been quite brief, lasting but a single night. Yet before leaving Ikarios' house, and perhaps without having made his identity known, he had left a vine-plant, promising the master of the house, a horticulturist by trade, that by following his advice he could extract from it an unusual drink. It was a time for mediations: the vine to be planted; the technique of vine-growing; the maturation of the fruit followed by the trampling of the grape and fermentation of the wine. Ikarios invited his neighbors to taste the new wine. The fragrance of the liquid amazed them. Before long they were singing the praises of the "wild mother's" fruit.[6] Suddenly one drinker fell over backward, another collapsed, and even the most robust teetered in drunkenness. Those left standing began to shout of murder and poisoning. They hurled themselves upon Ikarios and beat him savagely. His mutilated body was thrown into a well. His daughter Erigone hanged herself. His bitch Maira committed suicide, and the earth was afflicted with a terrifying sterility. When the voice of the oracle made itself heard, it exhorted those who listened to calm the dead but did nothing to establish the cult of Dionysos.[7] It was for mortals to drink uncut wine, the liquor that burned with

Inventing Wine and Distant Parousias

many flames yet poured out cold death, like the bull's blood offered in ordeals. In Ikarios' time wine was seen as a violent poison. Withdrawn into the shadows, Dionysos left it to man to discover the power of wine and of the god who inhabited it, never showing himself openly. The god of the banquet, the divinity that Tiresias heralded from Thebes, was to enter by another gate.

In the deme of Ikarion Dionysos wore the mask of the Stranger, the one worn by the gods when they went from city to city to observe "the excessiveness or equity of human actions."[8] And so Dionysos went as a night visitor, traveling in the land that still bears his name and where as early as the sixth century B.C. he reigned, cantharus in hand, in a temple that contained a marble statue of him nearly seven feet high. This Dionysos was closely associated with the Pythian Apollo,[9] and he would have seen Thespis, a member of the deme Ikarion, rehearse the choir, invent the speaking actor, and discover the mask shortly before triumphing in the Great Dionysia in the capital, Athens.[10] This was the theater through which Dionysos passed in so furtive a manner.

Forgetting Eleutherai

He had already left for another frontier, silently prowling about the gates of Eleutherai. There his actions became more complex, though he did not renounce the mediations offered him by the small village to the northwest of Athens whose name meant "Liberty." It was a border town, at the foot of Kithairon, on the boundary between the territory of Thebes and Attica.[11] And Dionysos was adept at revealing himself in more than one guise and cult site.

On the Theban slope was the mouth of a grotto,

distinct from the nearby temple of Dionysos Eleuthereus, the god who would eventually set out on the road to Athens.[12] The god of this cave—a god of possession—had a head covered with ivy.[13] A wooden column evoked another Dionysos, an inhabitant of the palace of Kadmos surnamed Perikionios[14] in memory of the ivy that miraculously covered the newborn to shield him from the fire that rained down from the sky. Behind the bacchant of ivy and wood erected in the open air lay the mouth of the cave in which Zeus, in order to seduce Antiope, transformed himself into a satyr[15] and companion of Dionysos. To this same cave came the Dionysian adept Dirke on her mountain thiasos.[16] And it was here, too, that a torture was prepared for Antiope in the form of a raging bull that ultimately turned against the queen of Thebes.

In counterpoint to the violent and ecstatic god of the Theban slope, however, stood the god of Eleutherai, who resided in the city's temple. The cult effigy of this Dionysos, transported to Athens, was used to inaugurate the cycle of the Dionysia. To commemorate its arrival, the Athenians on a certain date each year removed the statue of Eleuthereus to a relatively small temple located outside the city, not far from the Academy and close to a temple of Artemis.[17] At Eleutherai Dionysos, even in his urban temple, appears to have exhibited two faces, reflecting his two distinct native mediators. The first of these, eponym of the city, was called Eleutheris. He was a petty king with two daughters to whom fell the honor of discovering Dionysos carrying his beautiful black aegis. The girls thought he looked ridiculous, and the insulted god immediately afflicted them with his *mania*. Their worried father consulted the oracle and managed to put a quick end to their madness by decreeing an official cult in honor of

Dionysos of the Black Goatskin, the Melangaigis.[18] The god's brief anger was thus without further consequence, and this Dionysos seems to have been unaware of his Theban madness. Meanwhile the good Pegasos, a native of Eleutherai, had already set out for Athens with a single mission: to bring the Athenians the statue, the *agalma*, of Dionysos. This operation, though carried out in haste, nevertheless consisted of two stages.

At first the Athenians were hesitant. Dionysos received a cool welcome. Accordingly, the entire male population was afflicted with a kind of *satyriasis* and left in a painful state of erection that nothing seemed to alleviate.[19] Fortunately the Delphic oracle indicated the proper remedy: build a number of phalloi and carry them in procession in honor of the god heralded by Pegasos. The penile affliction mentally prepared the Athenians to devote to Dionysos a cult whose instrument and divine emblem was a large and handsome phallus. In Delos the phallus is referred to as the statue (*agalma*) of Dionysos.[20] Who can blame the people of Athens for being dubious about a strange god who appeared before them in the troubling form of a large, erect penis?

Following this first entry, a second embassy was crowned with success. Pegasos found a royal host. The groundwork for this triumph was laid by the priests of Delphi, who reminded the Athenians of the wine god's previous journey to the land of Icarus.[21] Dionysos' circuit in Attica ended with an official reception at the table of King Amphiktyon and with the gods of the city, undoubtedly those listed in a Delphic oracle that urged the Athenians not to forget Bacchus, the god of "ripe fruits" (*horaia*), as well as to form choruses, erect kraters, and burn offerings on street altars to Zeus Most High, Herakles,

Inventing Wine and Distant Parousias

and Apollo the Protector (Prostaterios), god of the altars placed before the doors of houses (Aguieus).[22]

Dionysos entered the city through the gate of the Dipylon, which opened onto the road used for great processions, when the entire city turned out to admire the spectacle of itself. Pausanias the Periegete saw among a profusion of multicolored statues in Athens one of King Amphiktyon receiving Dionysos along with other deities, with the sumptuousness of the Theoxenia in the temple of Pytho, of which Apollo was so fond. This was Dionysos in glory, completing the work begun at Ikarion on the day he left behind him the first vine-slip. At Amphiktyon's table Dionysos instructed his host the king in an art that he had not bothered to teach to his previous host, the master of orchards: that of drinking wine, of savoring the new drink that he had revealed to mankind. For clearly, as the events at Ikarion made clear, wine is not to be drunk without precautions.

Blood of Heaven, Blood of Earth

The traditions surrounding the grape and the discovery of the first slip reveal the supernatural origin of the vine, concealed in the story of Ikarios in which the emphasis is on the superhuman violence contained in the beverage extracted from its fruit. One day a drop of divine blood fell from heaven to earth. From it grew a bush with climbing vines, tendrils, and shoots. The wild vine, growing unattended (*autophues*), wrapped itself around trees in a sort of natural espalier. It continued to grow until Dionysos, wandering through the world, happened upon it and recognized in the grapes swollen with their dark red juice the fruit foretold in Rhea's oracles.[23] According to another version, it was Orestheus the Mountaineer, a king of Aitolia, who served as mediator. His bitch gave birth to a piece of wood instead of a litter of pups. Orestheus gave orders that this wood be planted in the earth, and from it grew the first vinestock. The king's bitch evokes the astronomical sign of the Canicula, the Burning Dog, Sirius, while King Orestheus had a grandson named the Winemaker (Oeneus) by his father, called the Planter.[24] Another version is that Orestheus himself, while driving a herd of goats, discovered the first vine by following an adventuresome billy goat who left the herd to graze in peace on the leaves and fruit of a shrub that clung to the bank of the Achelous. The goatherd returned from his expedition with wine as a gift for his master, King Oeneus, the sacred vinegrower.[25]

Stories about vinegrowing recapitulate the same transition between the savage and the cultivated, which in this case are indigenous and quite explicit categories. The growth of new branches is encouraged by pruning and trimming of the vine, accomplished by the grazing of the ass, which like the goat is a Dionysiac animal that voraciously consumes vineshoots.[26] Its jaw is a natural model for the curved pruning knife used for stripping leaves and cutting shoots after flowers have appeared to aid in the formation of buds. There is a pre-pruning Dionysos,[27] counterpart of the god who causes the vine to grow (Auxites) or the leaves to multiply (Dasullios). This is the Dionysos "of the cultivated vine," Hemerides, who prunes away the wild part of the vine, eliminates irregularities, and is adept at transplanting vines from the wild to the vineyard.[28]

When the vine metamorphoses into wine, the drink that a Greek physician called the "blood of the earth" must be tamed a third time (the invention of the vine being the first and its domestication being the second).[29] Born "of a savage mother," wine is a substance in which death is mixed with life magnified tenfold, in which burning fire alternates with a moistness that quenches thirst. It is as much a remedy as a poison, a drug that either enables man to outdo himself or turns him into a brute, that introduces him to ecstasy or plunges him into bestiality, like the Centaur lurching about the hall of the palace of Pirithoos. Wines of similar vintage and origin produce contrary effects: Theophrastos' *History of Plants* contains a chapter on the subject that is a classic of oenology.[30] The wine of Heraia in Arcadia makes women fertile, while drinking cerynia from Achaia or even crunching a grape can cause an abortion. Troezenian causes impotence, another wine, insomnia. The merest drop of a third brings insanity.[31] But the mysterious virtues of the dark red liquor are concentrated when wine of all varieties and vintages is mixed and drunk neat, unmixed with water. Left to itself, the must, or expressed juice of the grape, ferments rapidly. Since the sugar that makes fermentation possible is found in the seed, the fruit of the vine offers the spectacle of a fire that ignites spontaneously in the depths of a liquid. The wine "works," cooks by itself in the barrels, its surface agitated by its natural heat. It begins to boil. It is liquid fire in a jar, trembling at the breeze like Zephyr—he who brings fertility to mares—and sensitive to the movements of the great constellations above.

The igneous, fiery nature of wine is experimentally proven in the ritual of libation. Pouring it on the flames causes the fire to grow, as Theophrastos notes in his treatise *On Fire*.[32] The flames rise high into the sky when Alexander, passing through Thrace, has pure wine poured

Inventing Wine and Distant Parousias

on the altar of Dionysos.[33] The libation is appropriate to the nature of divinity, the dead, and the Good Genius who personifies its burning power. In the plays of Aristophanes,[34] to pour out a brimming glass of wine is to play Russian roulette: what ensues is either sudden death, as though one had drunk bull's blood,[35] or inspiration, as the Good Genius is awakened and one begins to prophesy, to become Bakis. Thunderbolts lurk in wine, and one must be struck by them before chanting the dithyramb.

In Paros Archilochos was witness to this. Dionysos flowed in his veins; he was *bacchiè*—the trance was in him.[36] Blood of the earth, blood from the sky, wine was the color of man's blood. It was also subject to the same alchemy, for within the organism it was transformed into a new blood. And when pure wine was mixed with the blood of an animal or human victim, it could be used to mark the most frightful of oaths: the league of the Seven against Thebes, for example, or the Kings of Atlantis before they donned their beautiful azure robes.[37]

Unmixed Wine, Akratos, was one of Dionysos' companions, a familiar figure in the thiasos. His mask is embedded in the wall of Dionysos' temple next to Amphiktyon's house in Athens.[38] He wears a frenzied face as a sign of Dionysos' power, the power that Amphiktyon agrees to moderate by explaining the proper use of the intoxicating liquid. How can it be made potable? How can it be turned into a drink that reinvigorates the drinker rather than knocking him out, rather than pouring bubbling madness into his veins? It is Dionysos' royal right to domesticate wine, to tame the mask of Akratos. Amphiktyon watches; he observes the god as he mixes the wine in the large vessel known as a krater, celebrating the first symposium and instituting the etiquette of wine-drinking.

Inventing Wine and Distant Parousias

By grace of Dionysos the word of Amphiktyon is henceforth the law of the banquet. After the solid food is eaten, that is, after the bread and meat, the host must offer each guest a taste of pure wine to demonstrate the power, the *dunamis,* of the Benevolent God.[39] The rest of the krater is to be carefully diluted, taking into account the number of guests, the place, and the season. Then the guests may drink as much as they like yet remain "safe and sound." The same ritual orders the feast of the Anthesteria, the most ancient celebration of Dionysos. In early spring the jars are opened. This is the time of the second fermentation. Each person must bring a barrel to the temple of the swamps (Limnai). There a libation of new wine is poured, and the god is asked to ensure that "the use of the *pharmakon* is without danger and salutary."[40] In other words, wine should be not a poison or a consuming fire but a remedy. For the remaining ceremonies, the only commandment is that the wine should be mixed.

The Strength of Wine

Here we have Dionysos as a civilizing god. Amphiktyon raised an altar to him in the sanctuary of the Seasons,[41] the Hours, the powers concerned with ripe fruits (*horaia*) and with the proper balance between dryness and humidity.[42] The new god was venerated under the name Right, Orthos: a Dionysos of the vertical, but also of correctness, rightness. An Athenian expert on the subject commented: "It was by drinking properly mixed wine that men ceased to stand in a bent posture as they were compelled to do by neat wine."[43] Amphiktyon's guest thus gave humanity its vertical stance. Compare this with Demeter's role in Eleusinian tradition: with barley and cereal plants she is supposed to have given men the strength to stand erect, to cease to behave as "tetrapods."[44]

The homology between Dionysos and Demeter can be elaborated with respect to food. Before mortals discovered wheat and bread, they lived on wild roots, vegetables, and fruits and were obliged to eat raw foods with extreme tastes. Theirs was what the author of *Ancient Medicine* called an "intemperate" diet.[45] In other words, they ate foods that could be described as *akreta,* which, like neat wine, caused violent pains, illness, and often sudden death. Just as well-tempered wine inaugurated "cultivated" life, so did Demeter's diet based on milled grains. Both deities inaugurated an art of living governed partly by considerations of diet, partly by culinary technique, and partly by medical knowledge.

Medicine was no stranger to the cooking of wine, any more than it was to the natural philosophy of the vine and vinegrowing. From the work of Mnesitheus, a physician of the fourth century B.C., we know of a Pythian oracle advising certain people—Athenians surely among them—to call Dionysos "dispenser of health" (Hugiates).[46] The god enthroned in the city of Athens was in no danger of being mistaken for his Theban cousin. A medical doctor and chief of the health department, model of righteousness and rectitude, the Athenian Dionysos was welcomed in good neighborhoods, to which he brought a reputation as a wise god who presided over the economy of needs and pleasures. In an irresistible ascension he rose from the outskirts of Attica to the summit of the politico-religious hierarchy. During the Anthesteria the queen, the legitimate wife of the first magistrate, of the king "responsible for all the traditional sacrifices," performed in conditions of utmost secrecy on behalf of the city certain sacrifices and ceremonies in the temple of Dionysos in the swamps (Limnai).[47] In the service to honor the god she was assisted by fourteen priestesses known as Elders (Gerairai) and cho- sen by the king. They swore a solemn oath to remain free of all taint, particularly that occasioned by union with a male. They also promised to honor Dionysos by celebrating the Theoinia, the feast of the Wine God, and the Iobaccheia, haunted by the ritual cry of the followers of Bacchus.

The most sacred of Dionysiac cult sites was open only one day a year. Here secrecy and publicity were combined in a unique way. On a stele erected next to the altar the rules of the ceremony were inscribed, and these have survived in the form of "half-effaced Attic characters." The ceremony was political, which was essential in a city governed by the requirement of publicity in all its temples. Nevertheless, in a place given over in its entirety to the leading *female citizens* of Athens, only the officiating celebrants were allowed to participate in and to see a ceremony whose nature they were absolutely forbidden to reveal.[48] On the appointed day the queen entered the Boukoleion, the ancient royal residence next to the Pryta- neum, where she married Dionysos in the name of the city.[49] Amphiktyon's guest on that day, in the presence of his immaculate priestesses, was made high priest of mar- riage and its offspring. In the shadow of the partly open sanctuary, the "Dispenser of Health" donned the mask of sovereignty over Athens and all its territory, a mask that no male eye was permitted to see.

In regard to honors the Athenian Dionysos had nothing to envy his counterpart reigning over the Kad- meia. But in his Attic journey as an epidemic God he offered the unprecedented spectacle of a deity of the vine and of unwatered wine gradually shedding his savagery, setting aside his wrath, and ending his murderous violence. He did so to the point where the inventor of the alcoholic drink was transformed into a patron saint of the tranquil life, of good health and marital felicity. Sublime actor, he sat, cantharus in hand, sipping tempered wine among the bourgeois and rentiers of the agora. And to cover his tracks even more, did he not go so far as to send the maenads and their disturbances away toward Parnassos, entrusting this mission exclusively to the Thuiades, elite bacchantes who every two years were sent off to join their Delphic counterparts?[50]

It is misleading to think of Dionysos exclusively in his Athenian guise, confined to a small town or banished to some forlorn spa. For the only stage grand enough for his leaps was the sea, the islets and the thousand inlets of the Greek coast. His dance floor was all of Hellas. The epiphanous god of fermented liquor did not fall asleep at Amphiktyon's banquet. And for every cantharus of watered wine, ten fountains of unmixed wine followed in his train. Through a series of cult sites Dionysos' parousia masked itself in the force of the vine, in the ebullience of liquor, in volcanic wine.

On his feast day, the appointed date of his arrival at his altars and temples, Dionysos often caused the vine to shoot up in a single day; he made wine bubble up ready to drink from the naked earth; and he caused the intoxicating liquor to boil in hermetically sealed barrels. He upset the regular progression of the seasons and interfered with the techniques of vinegrowing and winemaking.

There were two ways in which he liked to show himself in this guise, the first being in the form of "ephemeral" vines. In Euboia, on Parnassos, at Aigai, a miraculous vine appeared. It grew before one's eyes: leaves

Inventing Wine and Distant Parousias

in the morning, grapes in full bunches by noon, wine by evening.[51] A year elapsed in a day, and spontaneous vines proliferated in the wild, invading the slopes of Parnassos and intoxicating the rocky lair of Euboia. At Aigai the vine branches spread and sprouted their fruits even as the women formed choruses and celebrated the annual ceremonies of Dionysos. On that day unwatered wine flowed while the maenads—the chorus of married women initiated by Dionysos, his *mustides*—danced.[52]

Dionysos also appeared in springs and fountains of wine. Teos, Anakreon's birthplace and a city whose founder bore the name Dionysos, was also the birthplace of Dionysos according to residents, for whom incontrovertible proof was to be found in the fact that a spring of sweet-smelling wine flowed there spontaneously on certain days of the year.[53] At Andros in the Cyclades Dionysos' sanctuary was transformed into a fountain of wine on the day known as Theodosia, "gift of the god." But this wine turned to water if removed from the vicinity of its source.[54] It had to be drunk on the spot, with its bouquet of epiphany.

These miracles should not be classed in some vague way as marvels, as tales in a golden legend that has nothing to do with Dionysos.[55] They should be seen, rather, in their proper context, in relation to other new epiphanies, to other manifestations of the god as violent as the one that occurred in the palace of Thebes, even those whose geographical remoteness places them at the outer limits of the scope I have allowed myself in this book. Dionysos is an invitation to the exotic, and in this case he compels us to look to the farthest reaches of the Western world. But this detour will take us straight to the heart of his unique power, nature, and behavior.

Inventing Wine and Distant Parousias

3. The Island of Women

IT WAS in Gaul that Strabo, the geographer and contemporary of Augustus, discovered an unusual Dionysos who had previously attracted the attention of the philosopher and ethnographer Posidonius of Apamea.[1] In the land of the Celts beyond the Alps, Strabo, before embarking for Thule, painted in broad strokes a portrait of the Gaul: with long hair and baggy pants, he ate and slept on a litter of straw and produced salt fish much prized on the export market. He was, in short, a barbarian, one of a nation that exhibited to Strabo's eye the usual inversion of male and female labors, as well as any number of practices no less riveting than a custom described by Posidonius (who was at first repelled): warriors collected the heads of their slain enemies and hung them about their horses' withers. Druid philosophers, moreover, carefully observed the convulsions of sacrificial victims slain by swords thrust into their backs and from these observations derived highly accurate prognostications.[2] Immediately after this report, Strabo, who was apparently following right along in the well-traveled philosopher's ethnographic notebooks, recounts the strange behavior of a local Dionysos:

Posidonius affirms that in the Ocean there is a small island, which he places at the mouth of the Loire, and not altogether in the open sea. It is inhabited, he says, by the women of the "Namnetai," women possessed by Dionysos and devoted to appeasing the god by rites and all manner of sacred ceremonies. No male is allowed to set foot on the island. But the women, all of whom are married, cross the water to couple with their husbands and return to the island thereafter. Custom dictates that once a year they remove the roof of the sanctuary and replace it with another on the same day, before sunset, each one carrying a share of the load. Anyone who drops her bundle is torn to pieces by the others, who, crying the evoe, parade her limbs around the sanctuary. They do not stop until their frenzy (*lutte*) has ended. It never fails that one or another falls and is obliged to submit to such a fate.

A New Roof

This peculiar Dionysos, too Hellenic to be baptized "Celtic," is as embarrassing to geographers as he is to historians. Who were the Namnetai, whose name may survive today in that of the city of Nantes?[3] Is Posidonius talking about Batz or Dumet, islands in the estuary of La Vilaine about six miles offshore, or is he referring to Belle-Isle, despite its much greater distance from the coast?[4] In any case, the god's peculiar practices enable us to locate the island with some precision on the map of Greek dionysism.

Here we have a Dionysos caught between land and sea, an insular god who is apparently in sole command of his island, where he is surrounded by a congregation of ladies from Nantes devoted to his service. No male is permitted to land or reside on the island, as if it were the province of a god more misandric than misanthropic.[5] Though intransigent and puritanical, this Dionysos is a good administrator, for he permits his women, whom he has afflicted with madness, to discharge their conjugal duties on a regular basis—at home, of course, on the mainland. When not on leave, the island's women, all possessed, are fully occupied with serving Dionysos and attempting to curry favor with him through ritual and ceremony.

The god's first distinguishing characteristic is that his votaries are absolutely and permanently devoted to him. His women remain in his service for life. A second notable feature of this morose, not to say dyspeptic, Dionysos is that he requires his roof to be reconstructed once a year. The master of the house insists upon a new covering. But he is particular about the way in which his temple's roof is to be rebuilt. His women must take down the old roof and raise a new one in the space of a single day. Before the sun sets the new cover must be in place. With no time to lose, each woman carries her share of the load. And so it is that every year, infallibly, a rather surprising accident occurs. In the course of the work, one of Dionysos' women drops her bundle and falls. The accident would be harmless enough except that suddenly, as if all year long they had been waiting for the opportunity, the god's other servants hurl themselves on the poor unfortunate and tear her limb from limb, whereupon they parade her dismembered body around the temple, crying the evoe, until their frenzy ends just as mysteriously as it began.

How are the good sisters of Dionysos transformed

into maenads as furious as the Minyades and as ferocious as the mother of Pentheus? Why does Dionysos, on the day he receives a new roof, change from a grumpy rentier into Baccheus, the great god who mercilessly disseminates insanity? Two details of the narrative immediately catch the eye: the fact that the roof must be dismantled and replaced in a single day, and the fact that it is a falling body that triggers the trance and the ensuing madness. For a god to decide one fine day that the roof of his temple must be replaced is certainly out of the ordinary, especially when he insists that the work be completed between sunrise and sunset. A crackpot idea? A fantasy? It is particularly bizarre that it should come from a god who exhibits no particular interest in construction or architecture.

Dionysos generally prefers modest dwellings to sumptuous temples. The one god in the pantheon who is clearly an architect is Dionysos' brother Apollo, a veritable beaver, who at the tender age of four was already building altars, erecting walls, constructing his own temples.[6] In Delphi as well as Delos, Apollo planned his estates and assiduously improved his property. He was the founding god of two great cities and a bold promoter of colonial expeditions. His hymns are filled with the rumor of his activities: great and beautiful foundations, splendid walls, broad temple entries, impressive frames, imposing, heavy roofs.[7] At the beginning of the *Iliad* his priest Chryses, offended by the Greeks, reminds him that among other generosities of his priesthood he built a roof over the abode of Smintheus, the rat god of the Troad.[8] Compared to Apollo, Dionysos seems a rather humble suburban god, not to say a cave-dweller.[9] He travels from furnished room to furnished room, from simple house to modest sanctuary.[10] He is particularly delighted to find makeshift

The Island of Women

shelter, such as the lair provided for him in the sanctuary of Apollo during the Pythian Games.[11] To be sure, in the fourth century B.C. Dionysos was also honored with great temples, but his preferred dwelling place was of the sort he was offered somewhat later by a physician from Thasos: "A temple in the open air, an open-air *naos* with an altar and a cradle of vine branches; a fine lair, always green; and for the initiates a room in which to sing the evoe."[12] It is hard to take this deliberately nomadic god seriously as an architect.

Tripping

What about the second detail of the island ceremony, when one of the women carrying her burden trips and falls and the tenor of the scene changes so dramatically? In the world of bipeds nothing could be more banal than a fall, except perhaps when it occurs in the vicinity of Dionysos. In fact, there is much evidence to suggest that the foot or leg is a key part of the dionysiac body. Consider first Euripides' Bacchante, canonical in her happiness: regaling with evoes the god of the evoe, she leaps like a young mare, "she springs forward with a quick thrust of the leg."[13] Symmetrically, the tragic maenad Agave returns from Kithairon with "a bacchic step," drunk with murderous fury inspired in her by Dionysos and carrying Pentheus' bloody mask.[14] The bacchic step, the quick forward thrust of the foot, was taught to choruses of satyrs in Athens around 500 B.C. by the dancing master Pratinas, when he paid homage to Dionysos for an art threatened by boisterous imitators: "Prince crowned with ivy, note the movement of the right foot, its kick."[15] And when the god, wearing the mask of the foreigner, presides over the dressing of

Pentheus in front of the palace of Kadmos, he shows him how a bacchant must raise his right foot at the same time as he raises the thyrsus in his right hand.[16] This is the first of the Dionysiac gestures. More than once the god himself is invoked by his foot, as in *Antigone,* when his purifying assistance is requested so urgently to deal with the magnitude of the defilement.[17] And then, too, Dionysos is quite simply the god who jumps, who leaps (*pedan*) among the torches on the rocks of Delphi.[18] He capers like a goat among the Bacchae of the night.

In leaping Dionysos the foot (*pous*) encounters the verb to leap (*pedan*) and its form "to jump away from" (*ekpedan*), which is a technical term of the Dionysiac trance,[19] referring to the moment when the leaping force invades the body and takes control of it, carrying it irresistibly along. Aristoxenus, the musicologist from Tarento, has left a clinical description from southern Italy, between Locri and Reggio. The women were taken out of themselves: *ekstaseis.* Seated and busy eating, they thought they heard a voice, a call from afar, whereupon they jumped up (*ekpedan*), and no one was able to restrain them. They then began running away from the city.[20] To cure this epidemic evil Apollo recommended paeans, purifying chants, and spring songs, administered in a sixty-day course of treatment.[21] Musically, the result was a swelling of the ranks of composers of paeans.

There is no room for doubt. The Dionysiac trance began with the foot, with leaping—and in the Dionysiac world the ability to leap was the foot's most important characteristic. All who took part in the Dionysiac feasts, or, more precisely, in rural Dionysia, were familiar with a game that involved "walking" on one leg, that is, hopping. The game was known as *askoliasmos,*[22] reflecting the ancient meaning of a word that occurs in the story of the androgynes in the *Symposium*. These were cumbrous creatures with four arms and four legs, and the gods punished them by cutting each one in two. If they persisted in their arrogance, however, they were to be cut in two once again, forcing them to hop along on one leg (*askolizein*) rather than walk upright on two.[23]

Over the years, however, the etymology of the raised leg (*ana-skelos*) was lost. Insidiously, the *askoliasmos* was derived instead from the word for goatskin (*askos*) and its homonym. This etymology gained in prominence to the point where the hopping was forgotten altogether, supplanted by the swollen and slippery wineskin. It may be, however, that the custom of inviting drinkers to hop onto a greased wineskin was a distant echo of the forgotten etymology. For the amusement of those who remained seated on the ground, the contestants were obliged to leap (*pedan*, according to Didymos, the philologist with "brass entrails") to test their already compromised equilibrium.[24] It is easy to imagine that the homage thus paid must have gone straight to the heart of a god sometimes credited with having given the human race its erect posture. Before being initiated in the art of mixing wine with water, had not man gone reeling and "bent" under the inevitable effect of unmixed wine?[25] Thus, men hopped in honor of the god of Uprightness, Orthos, master of the art of properly mixing wine. So essential was this discovery to Dionysos that some, such as the theologians at Athenaeus' banquet, turning their attention from Dionysos to the drink that is the essence of divinity, maintained that the god of wine was truly *orthos*, "correct and insistent upon uprightness," provided the wine was properly diluted and mixed.[26] So Dionysos no longer caused anyone to totter; it was not he who made people fall.

Thus we have a Dionysos of uprightness as against a god of vacillation, which brings us to the third aspect of the pedestrian poser of the Atlantic coast. This time Dionysos appears in Delphi, as we saw at the beginning, with his cult enclave in the sanctuary of Apollo: a small sanctuary reserved for the god "who causes stumbling," Dionysos Sphaleotas.[27] This strange cult is hastily mentioned by Pausanias in recounting the story of a mask fished up from the seas in the net of a fisherman from Lesbos.[28] This is a Dionysos "who causes staggering," Sphalen or Sphaleotas, yet who is offered a sacrifice by Agamemnon "in the innermost depths" of the temple of Apollo, and who is mixed up in the prelude to the Trojan War, in the early history of the kings of Pergamon, and in the act of Telephos, king of Mysia.[29] Such, at any rate, are the credits engraved in stone in the first century B.C. by a pair of priests who served in his Pythian chapel.

The story is old. It begins with the blunder of the first landing. The augurs of Aulis predict victory, the Greeks embark, the fleet sets sail, and in the middle of the night the great armada reaches Mysia to the south of the Troad, convinced that it is landing near Troy. A night of confusion ensues. Hastily awakened, the king of the Mysians organizes the defense of the beaches. Achilles wounds Telephos, ancestor of the Attalids, who were very likely involved in the worship of a limping Dionysos. During the clash between the two heroes, in fact, Dionysos sneaks away. The god is irritated by the lack of respect shown him by the Mysians. His intervention causes Telephos to fall. Achilles' adversary catches his foot on a vinestock[30] and thus falls victim to a god already revealingly described

The Island of Women

by Lykophron as "Tumbler" (Sphaltes).[31] That night
Dionysos causes a vinelike shrub to spring up between
Telephos' feet. It shoots up suddenly (ex automatou) and
causes the king of the Mysians to topple over (sphallein).[32]
He trips on the vinestock. Out of the shadows emerges a
Dionysos who trips (huposkelizein). This is a variant of the
first ambush in the sanctuary at Delphi, but a variant explicitly claimed by the god of wine when he offers advice to
those who love him, to his companions of the krater. The
following passage is from a fourth-century B.C. comedy by
Euboulos entitled Dionysos or Semele:

> For sensible people I prepare only three kraters: one
> for health (hugieia), which they drink first; another
> for love and pleasure; and a third for sleep. After
> draining the third, those said to be wise go to lie
> down. The fourth I know not. It belongs to inso-
> lence. The fifth is full of cries. The sixth brims with
> insults and jests. The seventh has black eyes. The
> eighth is the bailiff, the ninth, bile. The tenth is
> madness (mania). It is this one that causes stumbling
> (sphallein). For poured into a narrow receptacle it
> easily trips up the one who drinks it (huposkelizein).[33]

Upright Dionysos stands aside after the fourth krater. If
the obstinate drinker collapses under his bed, the mania is
to blame. His reproaches should be addressed to the aptly
named Sphaleotas.

Spurts and Leaps

From the enthusiasm of the leap to the malicious tripping,
Dionysos conducts us along a route of his own to his island
kingdom, straight to the scene in which the women of the

island are seized with frenzy when one of them drops her
load and falls to the ground. One woman's foot is caught
by an obstruction, and the others' legs suddenly begin to
dance. The "roof-building" god turns out to be the
Stumbler as well, the god who trips as well as the deity
who makes dancers leap, who sends women into a trance
and from there into a murderous rage. The misguided foot
of the one is immediately answered by the frenzied leaping
of the others, the *ekpedan* that shakes the hardworking
congregation. Madness bursts suddenly onto the scene.
We have good reason to suspect that Dionysos has been
lurking about, awaiting the first misstep, perhaps even
quietly contriving to cause one of the women to trip. But
why does he want the women of Nantes to take down his
old roof and build him a new one? The alert reader may
already have formulated an answer, but in any case I shall
venture one of my own.

First, however, I must recall one important detail,
the urgent deadline: the roof must be repaired between
sunrise and sunset. One day: the time of the ephemera, as
one said in archaic Greece. The time that Dionysos
chooses for his epiphanies is nightfall, when the fading
light dispels the slow, deliberate gestures of works and
days and the patient techniques of vinegrowing. But is
not the god who, when toil is done, insists upon a new
roof (or, more precisely, a dismantling and reconstruction
of the existing roof) the same one who in the *Bacchae*
boasts of having driven all the women raving from
Thebes, forcing them to live among the mountain
evergreens without roofs over their heads (*anorophoi*)?[34] Is
he not the same Dionysos who rejoiced to live in a
beautiful open-air setting, the roofless temple at Thasos
given him by a generous physician?[35] Is he not the same

The Island of Women

Dionysos who slept under the stars in his round temple on a Thracian hillside?[36]

In reading the story of the island with its roof to be dismantled, how can we fail to recall that Dionysos presented himself in Thebes and Orchomenos as a god who joyfully set the roofs to dancing? The daughters of Minyas, barricaded inside their father's house, watched as its roof began to shake.[37] As Pentheus looked on in horror, the main beams of Kadmos' palace began to tremble and fall.[38] And Lykourgos' roof in Aeschylus' tragedy the *Edoni* was the first to "play the bacchant" as the royal palace literally "shook with enthusiasm" before collapsing in a frightful din.[39] All these tales suggest that there is good reason not to place too much confidence in Dionysos' talents as an architect. They are, moreover, excellent reasons to believe that once a year, perhaps on the occasion of an anniversary, this cloistered and morose guide might want to blow the roof off his island chapel. For a few hours, and with the complicity of his thiasos, roused from its lethargy, he became once again the god who caused his adepts to stagger, leap, and whirl, as he led them around his metamorphosed sanctuary in a terrifying and inward-spiraling masque. He was once more the Dionysos of frenzied women, who now carried in their hands not roof tiles for an ephemeral construction project but the quivering limbs of a woman torn to pieces before the eyes of a terrifying deity who randomly singled out victims for destruction. A patch of open sky glimpsed through a roof was an irresistible opportunity.

This was surely a peculiar parousia, even if it took place in the vicinity of other spattered blotches of red—the red of wine, this time, rather than human blood. But such haughty insolence revealed Dionysos as he really was. In refined and discreetly obsessional language the story of the Dionysos of the island reveals a god who could seem to be one thing all year long yet suddenly, on one particular day,[40] revert to his true self, reminding anyone who might have forgotten that he was none other than the Stranger within, the god who could turn anyone he pleased into fire and blood.

There is no mistake. The ephemeral Dionysos of wine has not strayed into the orgy of a savage and solitary god. The semantic homology between the two is quite rigorous. In Dionysian territory the same word was used to denote spurting wine and leaping maenads. In the *Bacchae* pure spring water "leaps" (*ekpedan*) from a rock struck by a thyrsus, just as wine flows from the spot where a bacchante has planted her staff.[41] And a woman stricken by Dionysos "leaps" (*ekpedan*), whether she is at home in her house, away in Kithairon amid oaks and pines, or obliged to do monotonous service in a temple.

Furthermore, the equivalence between the two topics of the Dionysiac parousia is confirmed by the common mark of the sudden and spontaneous, the *automaton*, another technical term of Dionysian epiphany. The bonds that hold the Bacchae fall away "of their own accord."[42] The vinestock grows up between Telephos' feet "in the blink of an eye."[43] At Teos and in the sanctuary at Andros the spring of wine begins to flow "suddenly, by itself."[44] And on the Atlantic island Dionysos' frenzy takes the form of an *automaton*, even if the word is not explicitly mentioned. Dionysos refers to himself as the sovereign master of the spontaneous and sudden. He appears in a surge of natural energy. Prince of immediacy, he is even a sort of fetish, adored as such by the workers of the earth. The presence of the elemental Dionysos can be recognized in the fact that a mere cutting, a slip stuck into the earth, begins to grow of its own accord in some mysterious fashion.[45] Thus we have the rustic image of a Dionysos *autophues,* an autonomous power whose natural energy suddenly bursts forth and which remains unintelligible, refractory to all classification.

Leaping and spurting: the connection between the two phenomena is evident in the rituals associated with certain Dionysiac feasts. Consider first of all the annual ceremonies at Aigai, celebrated by married women who have been initiated by the god (*mustides*). These maenads are carried away by the dance while the new vine grows heavy with ripe fruit and at sunset yields undiluted wine.[46] But the most harmonious blending of the twin figures of leaping and spurting is at Olympia in Elean territory. The feast there was known as Thuia, Boiling, and Dionysos was the protagonist in both series of ceremonies associated with it.[47] According to a tradition that is not without rival, Elis is supposed to have been the birthplace of Dionysos, and the first vine is supposed to have been discovered at Olympia on the banks of the Alpheos.[48] In Olympia powerful Hera reigned with her priestesses, but here she got on well enough with Semele's son.[49] In this crowded birthplace of gods, bristling with altars and sanctuaries, Dionysos found a theater for his epiphany. This took two forms: a bull leapt to be sacrificed, and wine suddenly filled the unopened casks—two parousias under the same sign, Thuia, or Boiling.

With its Bacchic eponym the feast links the two notions of leaping and spurting (*pedan-ekpedan*). Traditionally Thuia was the daughter of Parnassos, the first to lead the "orgies" of Dionysos.[50] In Delphi, however, she was also the Whirling One, Thuie, mistress of the great winds, whom the Delphians, frightened by the arrival of the Persians, called upon for help.[51] Also on Parnassos were the Bee Women who taught Apollo the art of divination:[52] their heads were covered with white powder, and when they had gorged themselves on yellow honey they began to buzz, became effervescent (*thuiein*), and spoke the truth, the whole truth, holding nothing back.[53] Finally, when Semele, a mortal, Thuone,[54] entered the precincts of Olympus, she became the first Bacchante, and those who touched her pregnant belly entered into a trance. Related to her were the Thuiades,[55] or Boiling Ones, women who were possessed by Dionysos, who is portrayed among them on one of the pediments of Apollo's temple. Those who came from Athens to celebrate the biennial ritual of Dionysos around the Korykian cave were the Leaping Ones, who paraded through the night. Those who came from Delphi to officiate mysteriously in the feast in honor of the Heroine were assigned the mission of waking Dionysos, the god "in the winnowing basket," asleep or burrowed in the ground near the oracle, while the priests known as the Pure Ones, the five Hosioi, completed a secret sacrifice in the temple of Apollo.

Effervescent: the god of the Eleans was "effervescent" in that city's sanctuary when solemnly invoked by the Sixteen,[56] the priestesses responsible for honoring Hera and for the costume that was woven for her every four years. "Come, Lord Dionysos, into the pure temple of the Eleans, come with the Charites, leaping (*thuon*) on a bull's clog."[57] Addressed twice subsequently as "Powerful Bull," the god, invited for the day of bounding and spurting, is supposed to appear in his animal form as a raging bull at the gallop, leaping with a single bound into the temple described as pure—a manifestation of the power of a god whose epidemic took place in the company of the Charites, deities of light and mothers of luminous joy.

In the same Elean ritual there was a second Dionysiac epiphany, in a house located some eight stadia from the city and under the protection of male priests. This involved a Dionysos of the fields, who was surrounded by both citizens and strangers.[58] The priests made preparations for the ceremony before a crowd in which Eleans mingled with outsiders. Three caldrons were carried into a room that was the counterpart of the temple of the Sixteen priestesses of Hera. Anyone could verify that the containers were empty. They were then sealed, as were all the entrances to the house. The next day, after checking that none of the seals had been broken, the priests opened the house of Dionysos, and the caldrons were found to be brimming with wine. The god had spurted,[59] and the wine had boiled in the barrels. Effervescence welled up from the depths of the native soil, overcoming all obstacles of construction as easily as it dispensed with the petty chores associated with the growing of grapes. "Cannot the gods pass through walls?" Dionysos asks Pentheus, who stubbornly keeps him under lock and key, with a roof over his head.[60]

The warning still holds good for the interpreter, Dionysos' present-day servant, who might otherwise place too much credence in Dionysos the "dispenser of health" and god of "Good Wine." His ejaculatory powers require the high parousias of his Elean domain or his island of women. Dionysos appears in his full glory in epiphanies in which the boiling fire of wine spurts with the same intensity as the bloody frenzy that drowns its prey, possessed and carried away by the dance. The leaping of the maenad and the volcanic eruption of the wine: in these perhaps we glimpse the nature of Dionysos, insofar as his powers of illusion are susceptible of autopsy.

4. The Heart of Dionysos Bared

𝕬 ANOTHER excursion into the history of semantic change will take us beyond "spurting and leaping" to a physiological mechanism fundamental to dionysism. Consider first a maenad's body, as described by Homer at the precise instant that Andromache has her intuition of misfortune—the death of Hector.[1] She gets up and "leaps" about the palace. "She is like a maenad," with a "palpitating heart" (*pallomene kradien*). Her maenad's heart beats a chamade, or *ciamada,* as the Piedmontese say, from the name given to the drum and bugle call by which the besieged inhabitants of a city informed their assailants that they wished to surrender. In Greek this dance of the heart was called "leaping," *pedesis.* It was a product of fear, when Terror rose ready to scream and the heart began to leap, to dance to an accompaniment of clacking crotala.[2] The heart stamped its feet on the diaphragm, dancing a wild round on the body's entrails.[3] In particular these palpitations accompanied the activities of the Corybantes, frenetic deities that whirled wildly about a possessed dancer.[4] In the Corybantes, in fact, "leaping" is revealed to be an essential ingredient of life itself, precisely in the degree to which the corybantic dance combines with the frenzy of the bacchic body. There is palpitation in the human animal, and the educator of the *Laws,* Plato the pedagogue, makes a theory of it, using the term "choreia" to refer to both dance and music, to the movements of both body and soul.[5]

Dionysos' sovereignty over festivals and over the righteous elderly here finds its physiological basis.[6] When the tiny human animal first comes into the world, it is naturally "all fire": incapable of repose in body or voice, endlessly crying, jumping (*pedan*) chaotically.[7] A newborn is a frenzied little animal, crying and gesticulating without rhyme or reason and imbued with an instinct to jump (*to kata phusin pedan*), always ready to jump or leap.[8] Without this instinct neither rhythm nor harmony would exist. Instinctively understanding this, nurses rock their infants, swing them back and forth, subject them to incessant movement.[9] The reason for this kinesitherapy is quite simple: homeopathy. Child or adult, we are all subject to fears, to certain weaknesses of soul, and "when mothers want to put fractious babies to sleep, the remedy they exhibit is not stillness but its very opposite, movement— they regularly rock the infants in their arms—and not silence, but a tune of some kind . . . Hence, when such disorders are treated by rocking movement the external motion thus exhibited dominates the internal, which is the source of the fright or frenzy. By its domination it produces a mental sense of calm and relief from the preceding distressing *agitation of the heart.*"[10] Thus the ingenious nanny, the "healer of Corybantic troubles," shares a power of the gods. Babies when rocked are "enchanted" (*kataulein*), as one might enchant a frenzied bacchant (*ekphrones baccheiai/oi*) by a combination of music

The Heart of Dionysos Bared

and dance.[11] This healing technique was practiced long ago in the Argolid when Melampous (in an unexpurgated version of the tale) sought to treat the mad Proitides by subjecting them to a cure of noisy, violent dances with a band of youths.[12] These were similar to bacchic dances, and the women were also referred to as *baccheiai,* bacchantes.[13] Along with undiluted wine, their homologous counterpart, they were given to mankind by a Dionysos wreaking vengeance on Hera for the good of humanity.

Plato chose this version for inclusion in the *Laws,* where Dionysos becomes a philosopher and almost a twin of Apollo. This is surely an intellectual's vision, but one which, in a discourse that is extremely attentive to the Dionysiac virtues, is based on an accurate physiological model, of which Plato is perfectly well aware. In the *Timaeus* he points out that there is a principle of palpitation in every animal.[14] It is an organ: the heart. As the source of the blood that circulates rapidly to all the members of the body, the heart is kept informed of all the humors, of the slightest movement of concupiscence. Posted as sentinel, the heart is subjected to a series of "palpitations" (*pedesis*) when the irritated parts swell under the effects of fire. When it begins to leap in paroxysm, the gods have prudently provided a relief: the lungs, bloodless and soft and pierced with holes like a sponge, against which the heart can beat as necessary to calm and cool itself.

The heart of the maenad has been palpitating ever since Homer's Andromache. In Dionysian anthropology the heart muscle is like an internal maenad in the body of the possessed, constantly leaping within.[15] It is an organ formed from the condensation of the blood that flows through it, the principle of life itself, first and last in the biological order.[16] Firstborn of the embyro, it begins to move before the other parts of the body. After death it is said to go on beating, disappearing last just as it appeared first. The palpitating heart is so intimately associated with Dionysos and his power that orphic theology made it responsible for the rebirth of the god put to death and devoured by the Titans. Hidden or spirited away from the murderers' table, the heart of the strangled child contained Dionysos whole.[17] This interpretation was limited to the renouncers and disciples of Orpheus, but still it should not be distorted into being somehow a precursor of the cult of the Sacred Heart when it seems to have been based on a belief shared by all Greeks.

Aristotle takes note of it in his *Treatise on the Movement of Animals*.[18] The heart, an organ blessed with autonomy, is a separate creature. It manifests its presence in spontaneous movements, in its own autochthonous vitality. It shares this privilege in full Dionysiac brotherhood with the male organ, the *phallos* so abundantly present in the god's parousias. For the phallus, too, moves without orders from the intellect. Its volume increases and diminishes. Made of tendon and cartilege, it can shrink or expand or fill with air.[19] Its autonomy, the biologist observes, is even more visible when "the power of the sperm spurts from it like a kind of animal."[20] Paraded "erect" (*orthos*) and "tumescent" (for which the Greek means to swell and to beat with strong blows),[21] the male organ manifests, at private as well as official festivals, the presence of the god who causes maenads to leap and unwatered wine to flow. Like the heart, the phallus signifies his potency.[22] It represents the potential force that can suddenly be liberated, as when the adepts from Nantes, "their hearts pounding on their diaphragms," hurl themselves upon one

60

of their number and then go leaping about the temple brandishing parts of her dismembered body.

Here the autopsy discovers what was perhaps most novel about a god whose power was not so much "power over others"—the *kratos* shared by the Most Powerful (Kreittones), the Olympians—as it was "capacity that one possesses in oneself," or *dunamis*. This was "potency" viewed in the light of its autonomy, its potentiality, as set forth by Aristotle in the *Metaphysics:* a "source of movement or change which . . . is in the same thing qua other."[23] One of the most immediate illustrations of the principle of "power" was in botany. When the Hippocratic physicians who wrote the *Treatise on the Nature of the Child* sought to demonstrate an analogy between the growth of a plant and the growth of a child in the womb, they explained the process in terms of the combined effects of the humor (*ikmas*) and the sap, which they called *dunamis.*[24] The earth was full of humors of all kinds; it was the nurse. The seed drew upon these humors, swelled, and grew. The humor forced the sap (*dunamis*) to thicken in the seed. It became a leaf and burst open the pod. Warmed by the sun, the humor began to "boil." It became the fruit, which fed on the sap, the "power" of the plant rooted in the soil.[25] *Dunamis,* both humor and sap, denoted a "vital liquid" of the same nature as that which Aristotle recognized in the autonomous heart and sex organ. As the humid principle responsible for increase and growth, *dunamis* or power was fundamentally responsible for Dionysos' limitless power over nature and its spontaneous growth, from the wild vinestock to the orchard and its cultivated fruits. In the Dionysia he received no more than his due when he was offered "the first fruits of all things."[26] There was something in Dionysos that placed him in the company of the Seasons, the Charites, the powers of exchange and circulation. Thus he reigned over the scintillating, vivifying humidity known as *ganos*.[27] His was a seminal power, but oriented and given purpose by what radically distinguished it from other natural divinities, even the most similar[28]—in particular, the spurting of moist, subterranean life, that which crowns the scale of vital humors, in boiling blood and frothing wine.

Confirmation of this can be found in the story of a companion of Dionysos by the name of Bryaktes,[29] whose semantic history can be traced to the same natural and vegetal roots. A relief from the fourth century B.C. (now in a private collection in Venice) shows Bryaktes lying at a banquet in the same position as Proxenos with the pointed ears on the heights of Delphi. Bryaktes is the Exuberant One. He shared in the exuberance that gripped the land of Thebes when at the sound of its god's voice it brought forth a profusion (*bruein*) of green smilax, and when it gave itself entirely to Bacchus by growing a cover of oaks and pines.[30] Think of the luxuriance of bryony, the wild vine.[31] In its root and etymon *Bryaktes* evokes a profusion of sap, a swelling, which evolved in one sense toward the word *embryo,* growth in the belly (but this has nothing to do with Dionysos), and in another toward exuberant growth, to life "springing up" out of the earth.[32] Two dominant figures recur once more: frothing, unmixed wine, which rises in effervescence to the surface of the cup,[33] and the leaping of the dancer, between Pan's animal leap at the entrance to the Korykian cave and the dance of Silenus, also crowned with heavy bunches of grapes that could make even marble dance.[34] The Exuberant One makes it impossible to interpret Dionysos as possessing a power somehow diluted in the bowels of the earth and thus to confound him with gods quite innocent of his *dunamis,* of his singular power, symbolized by blood and wine in a state of grace.

℞ What makes Dionysos run? What makes him jump and spurt? What drives him to appear under the sign of ejaculation? What is the nature of the power that is responsible for both the fountain of unwatered wine and the frenzied dance of women screaming the evoe and tearing each other apart? What is the brutal, sudden force that erupts in such different places and forms? Or, to put it in terms more appropriate to the polytheistic system and the complex of relations among gods and groups of gods of which Dionysos is fully a part, what is the unifying principle of his activity? What is his mode of action?

To answer this question we must penetrate the god's shimmering manifestations to identify the focal point of his means of action. We must look beyond the mask, the shapeless otherness of an obvious sovereignty over life and death. We needed a route to the summit: the god's "epidemic" drive, his need to appear suddenly, and his stubborn insistence on not being recognized. Dionysos, some say, may have had enemies. But no: he himself sets the stage upon which he will make his identity known. The stranger within, he causes his victims to lose their grip on themselves, to flay their own flesh, to rush headlong into defilement. High parousias.

Such a god does not reveal his line of attack while seated, lying down, or idle. Two settings were chosen. One was exotic, almost too bare: the island of women in the Atlantic, off the coast of Gaul. The other was so familiar that its features were blurred: Thebes, the palatial city in which Dionysos sat as a "political" god alongside

Apollo, just as both appeared at Delphi. In both places the god acted by causing his power to erupt inside the bodies of his followers, in their minds and members. In Thebes, his native land, his aunt Agave, her hands covered with her own blood, was banished forever. His grandfather Kadmos, so proud of having founded the city with Seven Gates, found himself condemned to a state of sacrilege, profaning graves and overturning the holiest of altars. Meanwhile, on the god's Atlantic island retreat, his devotees came unhinged once a year. The violence of their frenzy was all the greater because their affliction on this island of no escape was so gratuitous. Around them Dionysiac signs ran riot: an open roof, an unsteady foot, leaping, screaming, a dismembered body.

Dionysos in action, his heart laid bare: here we glimpse the innermost secret of his power, the power to cause spurts and leaps. Boiling blood and palpitating wine flow together to form a common principle: the "power" of a vital humor that draws from itself and by itself its capacity to liberate its energy, suddenly, with volcanic violence. Murderous frenzy, leaping maenad, effervescent wine, heart drunk with blood: all aspects of a single mode of action.

NOTES

INDEX

NOTES

1. Epidemic, This God

1. This is the version in Apollodorus, *Bibliotheca* 2.2.2, which the mythographer attributes to "Hesiod." Hera has her role in the madness of the Proitides, rivaling that of Dionysos, whom it is difficult to portray as a troublemaker in the house of Proitos and in the Argolid. On the Proitides, see F. Vian, "Mélampous et les Proitides," *Revue des études anciennes* (1965): 25–30; A. Henrichs, "Die Proitiden im hesiodischen Katalog," *Zeitschrift für Papyrologie und Epigraphik* (1974):297–307.

2. Herodotus 9.34; Diodorus 4.68: two versions in which the victims of the epidemic and its progress are the women of the Argolid.

3. "A disease, whether contagious or not, which attacks a very large number of people." E. Littré, *Dictionnaire de la langue française*, vol. 2 (Paris, 1869), p. 1459.

4. Cf. Jackie Pigeaud, *La maladie de l'âme* (Paris, 1981), pp. 218–225, with the analyses of *anapimplemi*, "to fill to the brim," and of terms denoting contact (*haphe*) and transmission by way of an organism (*diadidomi*). In an "Aristotelian" problem (I, 859 b 15) concerning plague and its power to contaminate on contact, one finds the image of fire, of a disease spreading like fire (*hupekkauma*). Pentheus refers to it in the *Bacchantae* (778–779): "At our very gates the frenzy of the Bacchantae rages like a fire, *pur haphaptetai*," as was noted by E. Rohde, *Psyche*, 10th ed., French trans. by A. Reymond (Paris, 1952), p. 297n4.

5. Rohde, *Psyche*, pp. 297–298.

6. Littré, *Dictionnaire*, p. 1460. The word is in the plural.

. See the bibliography in L. Weniger, "Theophanien altgriechische Götteradvente," *Archiv für Religionswissenschaft* 22 (1923–24):16–57, and F. Pfister, "Epiphanie," *Realenzyklopädie Supplement* IV (1924), c. 277–323. For a broader treatment see W. F. Otto, *Theophania: Der Geist der altgriechischen Religion* (Hamburg, 1956).

8. D. Wachsmuth, "Theoxenia," *Kleine Pauly*, V, 1979, c. 732–733. On the Theoxenia, a festival of the city of Delphi, see P. Amandry, *Bulletin de correspondance hellénique* 68–69 (1944–1945):413–415, complementing the *Bulletin de correspondance hellénique* 63 (1939):209–210.

9. According to *Scholia to Pindar, Olympiques* III, 1, ed. Drachmann, I, p. 105, 14–16.

10. Cf. A. Thivel, *Cnide et Cos?* (Paris, 1982), p. 33n60.

11. Ion of Chios in F. Jacoby, *Die Fragmente der griechischen Historiker* I (1922), etc. (hereafter cited as *F. Gr. Hist.* with the number assigned to each historian along with the fragment indicated by the reference), 392 F. 4–7. See also B. Gentili and G. Cerri, *Storia e Biografia nel pensiero antico* (Rome-Bari, 1983), pp. 74–75.

12. See the definitive analyses of W. F. Otto, *Dionysos: Le mythe et le culte* (2nd ed., 1933), 1948, French trans. Paris, 1969, pp. 81–92. On the arrivals of Dionysos see C. Kerenyi, *Dionysos: Archetypal Image of Indestructible Life* (Princeton, 1976), pp. 139–188.

13. The oracle attested by Pausanias 1.2.5 speaks of his *epidemic* in the time of Ikarios. "Epidemic" competes with "parousia" in Diodorus 4.3.3.

14. "Appearance" is an obsession in the *Bacchae*. See J.-P. Vernant, "Le Dionysos masqué des *Bacchantes* d'Euripide," *L'Homme* 93 (1985):39–42.

15. This is the key idea in H. Jeanmaire, *Dionysos, Histoire du culte de Bacchus,* 2nd ed. (Paris, 1970), p. 193.

16. To be sure, he is one of the Immortals (*Homeric Hymn to Dionysos* 2.6), even if he grew up in a cave and was born of a mortal mother, Semele, who though "a mere mortal gave Zeus

Notes to Pages 4–5*

an immortal son" (Hesiod, *Theogony* 942). Dionysos has to gain recognition only in the world of men.

17. This is the view of Rohde, *Psyche,* p. 296: "a kernel of historical truth." The cult of Dionysos came from outside Greece; it was a foreign cult. Along with Louis Gernet, H. Jeanmaire was sensitive to the proselytism, the propaganda, and the "missionary" figures of certain mediators of Dionysos (*Dionysos* 67, 85, 193, 355). Cf. L. Gernet and A. Boulanger, *Le génie grec dans la religion* (Paris, 1970), p. 105.

18. Interpretation of F. Robert, *La religion grecque* (Paris, 1981), pp. 101–107. A god with a plebeian heart, whose worshipers were supposed to have been sturdy ox drivers who engaged in the sport of *diasparagmos,* dismembering an ox.

19. *Bacchae* 556–575. With commentaries in J. Roux, *Euripide: Les Bacchantes,* vol. 2 (Paris, 1972), p. 435.

20. Pausanias 5.16.7. She was called Physkoa and was a member of the deme of Orthia in Elis.

21. Pausanias 2.7.5–6.

22. In the entry to Patras Dionysos was Aisymnetes and was associated with Artemis Triclaria. This raises problems that J.-P. Vernant has helped to resolve in the *Annuaire du Collège de France* 1982–1983, pp. 443–449, following the work of M. Massenzio, "La festa di Artemis Triklaria e Dionysos Aisymnetes a Patrai," *Studi e Materiali di Storia delle Religioni* 32 (1968):101–132, and D. Hegyi, "Der Kult des Dionysos Aisymnetes in Patrae," *Acta Antiqua Hungarica* 16 (1968):99–103. This epiphany is to be studied as one of the instances in which Artemis and Dionysos exerted a mutual influence on each other.

23. Apart from that of Patras. On Parnassos, Dionysian territory in Delphi, a proper name takes the place of a story. Pausanias 10.6.4: the daughter of an aborigine named Thyia becomes, without explanation, the first priestess of Dionysos and begins to celebrate her god's cult. Elsewhere Apollo marries her and fathers Delphos, a fine eponym for Delphi with its two great gods.

24. Pausanias 10.19.2. The English translation is adapted from Peter Levi, *Pausanias: Guide to Greece* (New York: Penguin, 1971), p. 454.

25. I am following a suggestion of G. Daux and J. Bousquet, "Agamemnon, Télèphe, Dionysos Sphaléôtas et les Attalides," *Revue archéologique* 1942–1943, I, pp. 113–125; 1942–1944, pp. 19–40 (esp. 31–33).

26. For *Kephalena* in the manuscripts, read *Sphalena*, now that the Delphic stele of Dionysos Sphaleotas (called Sphaltes by Lykophron, *Alexandra* 207) has been restored and deciphered.

27. Cf. P. Gauthier, "Notes sur l'étranger et l'hospitalité en Grèce et à Rome," *Ancient Society* 4 (1973):1–21.

28. Herodotus 8.144.

29. *Bacchae* 233, 247, 353, 441, 453, 642, 1059, 1077. But the women of his thiasos are of barbarian, Lydian, or Phrygian mountain origins.

30. Pausanias 3.16.9–11.

31. Ibid., 8.19.6–8.

32. As shown long ago by W. F. Otto, *Dionysos: Le mythe et le culte,* pp. 93–98 (the symbol of the mask) and more recently by Françoise Frontisi-Ducroux and J.-P. Vernant, "Figures du masque en Grèce ancienne," *Journal de Psychologie* (1983): 53–69; J.-P. Vernant, "Le Dionysos masqué des *Bacchantes* d'Euripide," *L'Homme* 93 (1985):31–58.

33. See P. Gauthier, *Symbola: Les étrangers et la justice dans les cités grecques* (Nancy, 1972), pp. 17–61. For a recent overview see M.-F. Baslez, *L'étranger dans la Grèce antique* (Paris, 1984), pp. 111–125 (with bibliography, pp. 35–36).

34. Gauthier, *Symbola*, pp. 41–52, which adopts the hypothesis of a sort of college, the "proxenes of Pytho," whose job was to welcome strangers in the temple. A colonist could become a "stranger" before the altars of the metropolis: for example, a citizen of Naupaktos in the fatherland, Hypocnemidian Locres. See L. Lerat, *Les Locriens de l'Ouest,* vol. 1 (Paris, 1952), p. 205; vol. 2 (Paris, 1953), pp. 29ff.

35. See M. Guarducci, "Bryaktes: Un contributo allo studio dei 'banchetti eroici,'" *American Journal of Archaeology* 66 (1962):273–280, plates 71–72 (reprinted in *Scritti scelti sulla religione greca e romana e sul Cristianesimo [Etudes préliminaires aux religions orientales de l'Empire romain,* 98] Leyden, 1983, pp. 10–19).

36. L. Lerat, "Reliefs inédits de Delphes," *Bulletin de correspondance hellénique* 60 (1936):359–361 (plate 44, 2). Reprinted in M. A. Zagdoun, *Fouilles de Delphes, 4, Monuments figurés et sculptures,* fasc. 6, *Reliefs,* 1977, pp. 23–31. For "Pan with cantharus," see P. Devambez, "La 'grotte de Pan' à Thasos," *Mélanges Paul Collart* (Lausanne, 1976), p. 123, fig. 5.

71

37. While awaiting the results of new research on thiasoi in Greece, one would not be ill-advised to reread Gernet's remarks in L. Gernet and A. Boulanger, *Le génie grec dans la religion* (Paris, 1932, reprinted 1970), pp. 106–109.

38. As in Aischylos, *Prometheus* 688 (words of "strangers") or Aristotle, *Rhetoric* 3, 1404 b 11 (on giving one's language a "foreign" coloration).

39. From which one of the two masks of the god of Naxos is made. See Aglaosthenes in Jacoby, ed., *F. Gr. Hist.* 499 F. 4.

40. Which it also is in, for example, traditions on the arrival at Semachos's. C. Kerenyi, *Dionysos: Archetypal Image of Indestructible Life* (Princeton, 1976), pp. 146–149. On the feasts of hospitality known as *xenika* see D. M. Pippidi, "Xenika Dionysia à Callatis," *Acta Antiqua Hungarica* 16 (1968):191–195.

41. Cf. C. Watzinger, "Thoxenia des Dionysos," *Jahrbuch des deutschen archäologischen Instituts* 61–62 (1947):77–87.

42. Euripides, *Bacchae* 219, 256, 272, 467.

43. Herodotus 2.145.

44. *Bacchae* 27–31: Kadmos' discovery, according to Dionysos. And Pentheus has his own version: 242–245.

45. While reaffirming that he is the son of Semele, whom he has just avenged and with whom he is so closely associated in Theban sanctuaries and a number of sacrificial ceremonies (for example, at Erchia, in the calendar of the fourth century B.C.: on the sixteenth of Elaphebolion, the priestess and married women sacrifice on the same day and the same altar to both Dionysos and Semele; meat for the women, the skin for the priestess). See G. Daux, "La grande Démarchie: un nouveau calendrier sacrificiel d'Attique [Erchia]," *Bulletin de correspondance hellénique* (1963):606, 609, 617, 619. On the essential relations between Dionysos and his mother, see Otto, *Dionysos,* pp. 71–80, and

77

Notes to Pages 11–13

P. Boyancé, "Dionysos and Semele," *Rendiconti della Pontificia Accademia romana di Archeologia* 38 (1965–1966):79–104.

72

46. These are the themes of the *Bacchae* (see J. Roux, *Euripide: Les Bacchantes,* vol. 1: *Introduction, Texte,* in French translation, Paris, 1970, pp. 106–107, frequently cited hereafter). For the history of the prologue and effects of the circulation of the text on its current state, see A. Dihle, "Der Prologue der Bacchen und die antike Ueberlieferungsphase des Euripides-Textes," *Sitz.-ber. Heidelberger Akad. Philos.-hist. Klasse,* 1981, II.

47. *Iliad* 6.130–143. Cf. Jeanmaire, *Dionysos,* pp. 60–67.

48. A rare term, also used to describe Achilles laying "his murderous hands" on the breast of the lifeless Patroclus (18.317).

49. Aeschylus, F. 69–81, ed. H. J. Mette. With commentary: *Der Verlorene Aischylos* (Berlin, 1963), pp. 136–138.

50. The sequel is in Apollodorus, *Bibliotheca* 3.5.1.

51. Herodotus 7.111.

52. A full bibliography may be found in J. Kambitsis, *Minyades kai Proitides: Ta mythologika dedomena* (Iannina, 1975). Less comprehensive is W. Burkert, *Homo Necans* (Berlin–New York, 1972), pp. 189–200. I cannot, however, accept Burkert's analysis, which neglects the defilement that afflicts the Minyades after they commit murder in their manic state.

53. Antoninus Liberalis, *Metamorphoses* X, ed. M. Paptho-mopoulos.

54. Aelian, *Varia Historia* 3.42. Plutarch, *Quaestiones graecae* 38.299 E–300A.

55. Porphyry, *De Abstinentia* 2.8. The Bassarai were adepts of "tauric sacrifice," but their Dionysiac vocation is a hypothesis that rests on two facts: first, that *Bassarai* in the feminine denotes maenads, and second, that the verb *haimodaitein* aptly describes maenads in the grip of mania like the frenzied Bassarai.

56. The form *Agrionia* is clearly attested in inscriptions pertaining to Thebes. See A. Schachter, *Cults of Boiotia,* vol. 1, University of London: Institute of Classical Studies, *Bulletin Supplement* 38.1 (London, 1981), pp. 185–192.

57. Plato, *Phaedo* 69 c = *Orphicorum fragmenta* F. 5, ed. O. Kern.

58. Euripides, *Bacchae* 39–49: *atelestos . . . baccheumaton.*

59. Argument of *Bacchae* 1.8–9.

60. *Bacchae* 6, 10–11. Cf. Roux's commentary, *Euripide,* vol. 1, pp. 242–243.

61. Amphiktyon's Delphic decree, E. Bourguet, *Fouilles de Delphes* 3.1, p. 198, reconstructed by J. Bousquet, "Les technites de l'Isthme et de Némée," *Bulletin de correspondance hellénique* (1961):78–85, and interpreted by L. Robert, "Les fêtes de Dionysos à Thèbes et l'Amphictionie," *Archaiologikè Ephemeris* (1977):195–210. The sanctuary of Dionysos Kadmeios is mentioned twice (16–17 and 27–28), as is the *hieron para ton sekon tes Semeles.* The parallel with the *Bacchae* is inescapable. Information on the inscriptions and texts may be found in Schachter, *Cults of Boiotia,* vol. 1, pp. 185–192.

62. Cf. A. Schachter, *Sophokles, Oidipous Tyrannos,* 210, in *Mélanges M. Lebel* (Quebec, 1980), pp. 113–117.

63. Proof is associated with the foundation of Messena, when Epaminondas and the Thebans sacrificed to Dionysos and Apollo Ismenios, associated in a couple homologous to that of Hera the Argive and Zeus of Nemea. See Pausanias 4.27.6. On Apollo Ismenios, see Schachter, *Cults of Boiotia,* vol. 1, pp. 77–85.

64. He completed his parousia by showing the Thebans that he was a god, a *great* god: Apollodorus, *Bibliotheca* 3.5.2; Euripides, *Bacchae* 183, 329, 770, 1031.

65. *Bacchae* 1296–1378. See also the fragments collected in *Christus Patiens,* ed. E. R. Dodds, 2nd ed. (Oxford, 1960), pp. 58–59.

66. *Bacchae* 1350, 1363, 1366, 1368–1370.

67. In the Roux edition, vol. 1, p. 219, l. 25.

68. Ibid., p. 217, l. 4.

69. Ibid., p. 219, ll. 26–29.

70. *Bacchae* 1314–1315.

71. Ibid., 1330–1338, 1354–1360. A pathological impiety, so serious a matter that the person obsessed with pillage was invited in Plato's ideal city to commit suicide. Plato, *Laws,* 9, 854 b–c.

72. Apollodorus, *Bibliotheca* 3.5.1.

73. Cf. *Bacchae* 55–60, where Rhea and Cybele are confused.

74. Callixenes of Rhodes in *F. Gr. Hist.* 627 F. 2 (particularly p. 174 of Jacoby, or Athenaeus 5.201 c). Cf. P. Goukowski, *Essai sur les origines du mythe d'Alexandre,* vol. 2: *Alexandre et Dionysos* (Nancy, 1981), pp. 81–82.

75. *Bacchae* 34: *skene.* Tiresias wearing the god's dress: 180. In this case, to "maenadize" seems homologous with "playing the bacchant," in the manner of Skyles in the streets of Olbia.

76. Ibid., 925–945. "Technical imperatives of a ritual embellishment," as J.-L. Durand and F. Frontisi rightly remark in "Idoles, figures, images: autour de Dionysos," *Revue archéologique* (1982):81–108 (especially p. 95). P. Boyancé, "Dionysiaca," *Revue des études anciennes* (1966) 33–60, has demonstrated the importance of clothing, the role of the belt, and the meaning of *katazosis* (see pp. 45–53) from the *Bacchae* to the Tusculum inscription.

77. *Bacchae* 851–853.

78. Ibid., 472. The *arrheta,* which only the *abaccheutoi* are permitted to know, accurately prefigure the "telestic" dimension (in Plato's sense) of Dionysiac ceremonies. I agree with Boyancé, "Dionysiaca," that interpretations that take no account of this testimony and of other contemporaries are to be rejected.

79. *Bacchae* 470. There is no proof that this type of experience relates directly to the trance or collective *orgia,* as J.-P. Vernant seems to suggest in "Le Dionysos masqué des *Bacchantes* d'Euripide," *L'Homme* (1985):42. Instead we are probably in the semantic realm defined by the double meaning of *bacchos/baccheus.* See J.-L. Perpillou, *Les substantifs grecs en "eus"* (Paris, 1973), pp. 315–316. The same term was used for both "celebrant" and "celebrated." W. Burkert, arguing against M. L. West, has established the Dionysiac connotations of this in "Le laminette auree: da Orfeo a Lampone," in *Orfismo in Magna Grecia* 1975 (published in 1979), p. 90, concerning the Hipponium tablet of the early fourth century B.C., attesting the existence of *mustai kai bacchoi,* the recipients of these written viaticums. The *bacchos* question has since been reconsidered in a convincing essay by S. Guettel Cole, "New Evidence for the Mysteries of Dionysos,"

Greek, Roman and Byzantine Studies 21 (1980):223–238. *Bacchoi* and *mustai* are placed under the sign of the *musteria* and *meuin* in the fragment on the night prowlers, attributed to Heraclitus (F. 14, ed. Bollack and Wissmann).

80. Plato, *Laws* II, 672 b 2–7. Figure evoked at the beginning of Euripides' *Cyclops* (3–4).

81. *Laws* II, 666 a–b. Cf. 671 d–e.

82. The cathartic dimension has been investigated by P. Boyancé, *Le culte des Muses chez les philosophes grecs* (Paris, 1970), pp. 63–66.

83. Sophocles, *Antigone* 1140–1145, cited in trans. by Elizabeth Wyckoff in D. Greene and R. Lattimore, eds., *The Complete Greek Tragedies: Sophocles, I* (Chicago: The University of Chicago Press, 1954).

84. Pausanias 9.16.6.

85. Photius, s.v. *Lusioi teletai,* with Heraclides Ponticus, F. 155, ed. Wehrli.

86. Pausanias 2.7.5–6.

87. Ibid.

88. Ibid., 2.2.6–7.

89. According to Athenaeus 3.78 c (= Aglaosthenes in *F. Gr. Hist.* 499 F. 4, ed. Jacoby).

2. *Inventing Wine and Distant Parousias*

1. Showing that the god of Thebes was perceived in opposition to the Athenian Dionysos.

2. Euripides, *Bacchae* 274–285. Echoing this are the Lydians in 381–385; the messenger repeats the wine god's theology in a less noble version (770–774). The English translation is by William Arrowsmith in David Greene and Richmond Lattimore, eds., *The Complete Greek Tragedies: Euripides, V* (Chicago: The University of Chicago Press, 1959), p. 166.

3. *Bacchae* 328–329.

4. Apollodorus, *Bibliotheca* 3.14.7.

5. Pausanias 1.2.5. The deme of Ikaria has yielded invaluable information about the complicity between Apollo and Dionysos, apparently including the remains of a great cult statue

of Dionysos with cantharus. See Irene Bald Romano, "The Archaic Statue of Dionysos from Ikarion," *Hesperia* 51 (1982):398–409 (pl. 93–95).

6. Aischylos, *Persians* 614.

7. I am summarizing here the long version in Hyginus, *Astronomica* 2.4, ed. Bunte, pp. 34–38.

8. *Odyssey* 17, 483–487; Plato, *Sophist* 216 a–b.

9. See n. 5 above and the inscription from 525 B.C. found near Python, which associates the two gods: D. M. Robinson, "Three New Inscriptions from the Deme of Ikaria," *Hesperia* 17 (1948):141–143.

10. On Thespis see *Tragicorum graecorum fragmenta*, vol. 1, 1971, ed. B. Snell, pp. 61–64.

11. Pausanias 1.38.8–9.

12. Pausanias 1.29.2.

13. Euripides, *Antiope*, F. 37, ed. J. Kambitsis (Athens, 1972), commentary on pp. 85–86.

14. Mnaseas, F. 18, ed. Müller. Cf. O. Kern, "Dionysos Perikionios," *Jahrbuch des kaiserlich deutscher archäologischen Instituts* 11 (1896):113–116.

15. F. 31, ed. Kambitsis.

16. Pausanias 9.17.5; see also the comments on Dirke's arrival in the introduction to F. 31, ed. Kambitsis, pp. xvii–xviii.

17. Pausanias 1.29.2. In the fourth century B.C. this was an important activity in the religious calendar of ephebes. See C. Pelekidis, *Histoire de l'éphébie attique des origines à 31 avant notre ère* (Paris, 1962), pp. 239–247.

18. Souda, s.v. *Melan.*

19. *Scholia to Aristophanes, Acharnians,* 243, ed. N. G. Wilson, 1975, pp. 42–43. Much more remarkable is the version in *Scholia to Lucian, Dialogue of the Gods,* 5, ed. Rabe, p. 211, l. 14, to p. 212, l. 18, in which Dionysos in the guise of a desirable ephebe takes it upon himself to arouse the men's desire, as punishment for the death inflicted upon Ikarios.

20. P. Bruneau, *Recherches sur les cultes de Delos* (Paris, 1970), pp. 314–317.

21. Pausanias 1.2.5–6.

22. Two oracles cited by Demosthenes, 21, 51; 43, 66.

Numbers 282 and 283 of H. W. Parke and D. E. W. Wormell, *The Delphic Oracle*, vol. 2 (Oxford, 1956), pp. 114–115.

23. Nonnos, *Dionysiaca* 12, 293–397.

24. Hecataeus of Miletus, *F. Gr. Hist.* 1 F. 15, ed. Jacoby.

25. *Mythographi vaticani*, 1, 87, ed. Bode, p. 30.

26. Pausanias 2.38.3: the ass of Nauplia.

27. *Scholia to Lykophron*, 577, ed. Scheer, p. 199, 9–16.

28. Plutarch, *Moralia* 12, 451 c.

29. Androcydes, cited by Pliny, *Natural History* 14.58.

30. Which has its experts, even if they are not well known: Pliny, *Natural History* 14.120, ed. J. André, n. 1, p. 139.

31. Theophrastos, *Hist. plant.* 9, 18, 10–11. Cf. Pliny, *Natural History* 14.116–117.

32. Theophrastos, *De igne* 65, ed. Wimmer.

33. Suetonius, *Augustus* 94.7.

34. Aristophanes, *Knights* 85, 105–106.

35. Cf. A. Touwaide, "Le sang de taureau," *L'Antiquité classique* 48 (1979):5–14.

36. Archilochos, F. 194, ed. West.

37. Aischylos, *Seven against Thebes* 42–48; Plato, *Critias* 120 a–b.

38. Pausanias 1.2.5; Athenaeus 2.9.39 c: in Sparta, the cooks-butchers-sacrificers rendered a cult to the hero Keraon, the Mixer, similar to the Kneader.

39. Philochorus in *F. Gr. Hist.* 328 F. 5 b, ed. Jacoby.

40. Plutarch, *Table Talk* 3.7.655 e.

41. Philochorus in *F. Gr. Hist.* 328 F. 173, ed. Jacoby.

42. Cf. M. Detienne, *Les jardins d'Adonis*, 2nd ed. (Paris, 1979), pp. 206–211 (published in English as *The Gardens of Adonis*, trans. J. Lloyd, Atlantic Highlands, N.J., 1977).

43. Philochorus in *F. Gr. Hist.* 328 F. 5 b, ed. Jacoby.

44. Previously humanity moved about on four paws. With the advent of barley, man stood up and competed in races in the stadium, a word derived from *stasis*, for vertical posture: see *Scholia to Pindar's Olympics* 9, 150 a–b, ed. Drachmann, I, p. 301, 21; p. 302, 4.

45. *L'Ancienne Médecine*, vol. III, ed. A. J. Festugière (Paris, 1948), pp. 37–38, on the notion of *kresis*. Demeter is of course

absent from this discussion; in this literature it is physicians who invent dietetics.

46. Mnesitheus, F. 41r and 42, ed. J. Bertier. A contemporary of Plato, Mnesitheus composed a body of medical work entirely devoted to dietetics, childrearing, and instruction on the use of wine as food. J. Bertier, *Mnesitheus et Dieuchès* (Leyden, 1972), pp. 29–147.

47. Demosthenes, *Against Neaira* 73–78.

48. Ibid., 76 and 79.

49. Aristotle, *Constitution of Athens* III, 5. On the Anthesteria from this point of view, see P. Carlier, *La royauté en Grèce avant Alexandre* (Strasbourg, 1984), pp. 331–335.

50. A. Henrichs pertinently observes that ritual maenadism was not practiced in Attica. He further notes that the consumption of wine in the Anthesteria had a social function, intended to strengthen social ties. See "Changing Dionysiac Identities," in Ben F. Meyer and E. P. Sanders, eds., *Jewish and Christian Self-Definition,* vol. 3 (London, 1982), pp. 141 and 153. Furthermore, it was in Eleusis, on the periphery of Athenian influence, that Dionysos cultivated his "telestic" dimension.

51. Texts concerning Sophocles, F. 255, ed. Radt, *Tragicorum graecorum fragmenta,* vol. 4, 1977, pp. 242–243.

52. Euphorion, F. 100, ed. Powell.

53. Diodorus 3.66.

54. Pausanias 6.26.1; Pliny, *Natural History* 2.231, 31.6.

55. I wish to pay tribute here to Michèle Gay of the Ecole Normale Supérieure of Sèvres for having been the first to explore these traditions in connection with research on "Dionysiac space."

3. The Island of Women

1. Posidonius in Strabo 4.4.6 = F. Gr. Hist. 87 F. 56, ed. Jacoby (= F. 34, ed. W. Theiler, vol. 2, p. 51).

2. Strabo 4.4.3–5. Another version, involving women alone on an island, is in the *Periegesis* of pseudo-Dionysus, 571ff. They perform the usual ceremonies for Dionysos, by night and

covered with ivy. There is a tumult of some sort, but the essence of the matter is obscure.

3. According to M. Leglay, s.v. *Namnetae,* in *Der Kleine Pauly,* vol. 3, 1979, c. 1565.

4. Cf. the geographical remarks of Fr. Lasserre in his annotated edition of Strabo, *Géographie,* vol. 2, *Collection des Universités de France* (Paris, 1966), pp. 215–216.

5. Males were excluded from a series of Dionysiac sanctuaries and ceremonies, to which only women were admitted. The converse was not true. A god whose presence is indicated by a *phallos* is not necessarily "phallocratic" or chauvinist. This will surprise no one, or perhaps I should say, virtually no one.

6. Activities that fill the *Homeric Hymn* as well as that of Callimachus.

7. Cf. G. Roux, "Testimonia Delphica II: Note sur l'Hymne homérique à Apollon, vers 298," *Revue des études grecques* 79 (1966):1–5.

8. *Iliad* I, 39.

9. Cf. in general P. Boyancé, "L'antre dans les mystères de Dionysos," *Rendiconti della Pontificia Accademia romana di Archeologia* 33 (1960–1961):107–127; D. M. Pippidi, "Grottes dionysiaques de Callatis," *Scythica minora* (Bucharest-Amsterdam, 1975), pp. 142–149.

10. "Soldiers" on patrol, *peripoles,* erecting a tent of leaves and consecrating an effigy of Dionysos: L. Robert, "Péripolarques," *Hellenica* 10 (1955):283–291; J. and L. Robert, *Bulletin épigraphique,* 1973 (*Revue des études grecques*), n. 260, pp. 110–111. A clearing, a pike stuck into the earth, a cavern on the mountain, an isolated cave, a simple house: the god of the theater loves changes of set, including monumental temples.

11. Philodamos, *Paean,* c. XI, 136–140, ed. Powell.

12. Cf. J. Pouilloux, *Guide de Thasos* (Paris, 1968), p. 172.

13. Euripides, *Bacchae* 166–167.

14. Ibid., 1230.

15. *Hyporchemus,* F. 1, ed. Diehl. For the musical ethic of Pratinas, see F. Lasserre, *Plutarque: De la musique* (Lausanne, 1954), pp. 45–47.

16. *Bacchae* 941–943.

17. Sophocles, *Antigone* 1140–1152.

18. Euripides, *Ion* 714–717, 1122–1126; F. 752, 2nd ed., ed. Nauck. Festival of Torches, Daidophoria, in the midst of the Thyiades.

19. Along with other verbal figures (*thoazein, skirtan*), which evoke the goat-god, Pan, who leaps with Dionysos around the Korykian lair.

20. Aristoxenus, F. 117, ed. F. Wehrli.

21. Pythagoras' conciliatory paeans are heard in the vicinity. But here Apollo and Dionysos interfere. Through its female population an entire city is menaced: a state of *loimos*. Apollo the founder is also the purifier, especially in Pythagorean territory.

22. See K. Latte, "Askoliasmos," *Hermes* 85 (1957):385–391; J. Taillardat in his edition of Suetonius, *Des termes injurieux, des jeux grecs* (Paris, 1967), p. 71 and pp. 170–171. I am indebted to Jean-Pierre Vernant for having suggested that I pursue this trail.

23. Plato, *Symposium* 190 d.

24. Cf. Didymos in *Scholia to Oribasius*, 44, 27, 12, p. 155, 23, ed. Raeder (see Latte, "Askoliasmos," p. 387).

25. Philochorus in *F. Gr. Hist.* 328 F. 5 b, ed. Jacoby (= Athenaeus 2.7.38 c–d). Dionysos "correct and vertical" is installed by Amphiktyon in the sanctuary of the Seasons (Horai).

26. Athenaeus 5.179 e.

27. On Dionysos as a god who causes stumbling, see G. Daux and J. Bousquet, "Agamemnon, Télèphe, Dionysos Sphaléôtas et les Attalides," *Revue archéologique* 1942–1943, I, pp. 113–125; II, pp. 19–40. Cf. G. Roux, *Delphes: Son oracle et ses dieux* (Paris, 1976), pp. 181–183.

28. Mask consecrated at Delphi: this was Dionysos Sphalen. Cf. n. 24.

29. Telephos: F. Jouan, *Euripide et la légende des Chants Cypriens* (Paris, 1966), pp. 222–255; and on the role of Dionysos in the Cyprian Songs, see A. Severyns, *Le cycle épique dans l'école d'Aristarque* (Paris, 1928), pp. 293–294.

30. Version collected in Daux and Bousquet, "Agamemnon," I, pp. 115–116.

31. Lykophron, *Alexandra* 207.

32. *Scholia to Lykophron,* 206, ed. Scheer, p. 96, 24–25. The Dionysiac sense of this intervention was noticed by Carl Robert. But G. Daux's common sense slipped (Daux and Bousquet, "Agamemnon," p. 118).

81

33. Euboulos, F. 94, ed. Hunter.

34. Euripides, *Bacchae* 38. In 684–686 we see them sleeping.

35. Cf. note 12, Chapter 3. In Laconia, at Brysai, the effigy of Dionysos was in the open air (Pausanias 3.20.3).

36. Macrobius, *Saturnalia* 1.18 (= Alexander Polyhistor in *Fragmenta historicorum graecorum,* ed. Müller, III, p. 244).

37. Ovid, *Metamorphoses* 4.402.

38. Euripides, *Bacchae* 586–593. Dionysos attacked the bearing structures: he amused himself by causing the "central beam" to shake. Pentheus spoke gravely of "his roof" and said that if Dionysos set foot under it he would have his head cut off (*Bacchae* 239–241). The shameless female followers of the curled and perfumed god he locked up under the "roof" of the public prison (227).

39. Aeschylus, F. 76 a and b, ed. H. J. Mette: *baccheuei stege.*

40. The sanctuary of Dionysos Lysios at Thebes was opened once a year (Pausanias 9.16.6). Here the entire island became Dionysos' sanctuary. He was a god-mask, around whom his possessed followers, brutally reawakened, began to dance.

41. *Bacchae* 704 and 711.

42. Ibid., 447 (*automata*).

43. Cf. n. 32, Chapter 3.

44. Pausanias 6.26.1. In Teos, the wine spring began to flow *automatos* in the city: Diodorus 3.66.

45. Maximus of Tyre 8.1. Dionysos caused orchards to grow; he was the god of sap, leaves, and ripe fruits.

46. Cf. n. 52, Chapter 2.

47. M. P. Nilsson, *Griechische Feste von religiöser Bedeutung* (1906; reprinted Stuttgart, 1957), pp. 291–293.

48. Theopompus in *F. Gr. Hist.* 115 F. 277, ed. Jacoby, and Diodorus 3.66. But his cult was introduced by Physkoa, his lover, accompanied by his son: Pausanias 5.16.6.

49. Cf. H. Jeanmaire, "Dionysos et Héra," *Annuaire de l'Ecole pratique des Hautes Etudes: Section des sciences religieuses*

Notes to Pages 50–54

(1945–1947), Paris, 1946, pp. 87–100; *Dionysos: Histoire du culte de Bacchus* (Paris, 1951), pp. 215–216; C. Calame, *Les choeurs des jeunes filles en Grèce archaique,* vol. 1 (Rome, 1977), pp. 210–214.

50. Pausanias 10.6.4.

51. Herodotus 7.178.

52. There is said to have been an Apollo Thuios at Miletus in the land of the god of choristers, of organized Molpoi (cf. Hesychios, s.v. Thuios).

53. *Homeric Hymn to Hermes* 560. Cf. S. Scheinberg, "The Bee Maidens of the 'Homeric Hymn to Hermes,'" *Harvard Studies in Classical Philology* 83 (1979):1–28.

54. Aischylos, F. 358, ed. Mette; Diodorus 4.25.4. According to Hesychios, there was a Dionysos Thuonidas at Rhodes, a god with *phalloi* of fig wood. An inscription from Chalcis, published and interpreted by Paul Veyne, "Une inscription dionysiaque peu commune," *Bulletin de correspondance hellénique* 109 (1985):621–624, has revealed a "thuonophore," or phallus bearer. Dionysos' ejaculatory power is manifested with the same joy in the whirling body of the possessed female and in the tumescent male organ, swollen with semen.

55. Pausanias 10.19.4; Plutarch, *Quaestiones graecae* 12.293 d–e; *Isis and Osiris* 35.365 a. Cf. G. Roux, *Delphes: Son oracle et ses dieux* (Paris, 1976), pp. 178–180.

56. Sixteen matrons, wives as respectable as the ladies who waited on the Queen of the Anthesteria. Every four years they wove a veil for Hera. Cf. Calame, *Les choeurs,* pp. 210–213, 244–245.

57. Plutarch, *Quaestiones graecae* 36.299 a–b, with commentary by W. R. Halliday (1928), pp. 152–157. The participle *thuon* is in perfect accord with the name of the holiday, Thuia (following the well-established alternation *thuein/thuiein:* P. Chantraine, *Dictionnaire étymologique de la langue grecque,* vol. 2, Paris, 1970, s.v. *thuo*), but has sometimes been corrected to *duon.* The text originated by E. Diehl and circulated by D. Page has led to interpretations like that of C. Béard in *Mélanges Paul Collart* (Lausanne, 1976), pp. 61–73 (especially pp. 70–71).

58. Pausanias 6.26.1–2. This feast differs from the first in a number of points: feminine/masculine as to the officiants;

city/periphery; temple/house; citizens/foreigners *and* citizens. Here we see once again the god of the *xenoi*, who likes to "mix" socially. In the Anthesteria the slaves participate in the festival. However, for the "unsayable," reserved for the Queen, males and foreigners are strictly prohibited.

59. As one sees him on his abductors' ship: *Homeric Hymn to Dionysos* 35–37.

60. Euripides, *Bacchae* 654.

4. The Heart of Dionysos Bared

1. *Iliad* 22.460. Does the maenad's body have a sex? The Corybant who takes his place in Plato's *Symposium,* 215 e 2, changes easily from one sex to the other. What sex is a heart (the noun is feminine in Greek)?

2. Aischylos, *Choephoroi* 1024–1025.

3. *Prometheus* 881 and *Agamemnon* 997.

4. Plato, *Symposium* 215 e 2; see also Ivan M. Linforth, "The Corybantic Rites in Plato," *University of California Publications in Classical Philology,* 13, no. 5 (1946):121–162.

5. Plato, *Laws* II, 672 e 5–673 a 10.

6. Plato, *Laws* II, 665 b; 666 a; 671 e; 672 d.

7. Ibid., 664 e 4–6. Cf. 653 d 7–e 3.

8. Ibid., 672 c 4–5 and 673 d 1.

9. Ibid., VII, 790 c 7–10.

10. Ibid., 790 e 8–791 a 6.

11. Ibid., 790 d 4–e 4.

12. Apollodorus 2.2.2, with an *entheos choreia.*

13. Version placed in *Laws* II, 672 b 3–5 at the beginning of the discussion of the choreia. Cf. n. 80, Chapter 1.

14. Plato, *Timaeus* 70 c 1.

15. The path explored by the physicians led from palpitation to beating in the body to the discovery of the pulse, attributed to Herophilus, the anatomist. See J. Pigeaud, "Du rythme dans le corps: Quelques notes sur l'interprétation du pouls par le médecin Hérophile," *Bulletin de l'Association G. Budé,* 1978, pp. 258–267 (the model is prosody).

16. Aristotle, *On the Generation of the Animals* III, 4, 740 a

3–5; the bloody spot that forms in the white of the egg palpitates (*pedan*) and moves: it is the heart: *History of the Animals* VI, 3, 561 a 10–13. As for *palpitation, pedesis,* it is analyzed in *Parva Naturalia* (479 b 19–480 a 15) by analogy with boiling or with an abscess on the point of breaking.

17. Cf. M. Detienne, *Dionysos mis à mort,* 2nd ed. (Paris, 1980), pp. 191–196.

18. 703 b 3–26.

19. Aristotle, *Parts of Animals* IV, 11, 689 a 20–31.

20. Aristotle, *Treatise on the Movement of Animals* 703 b 26: the *dunamis* of the sperm. Think, too, of the bird-phalloi on various ancient vases.

21. *Orthos, esphudomenos* (similar to *sphuzein,* from *sphugmos,* the "pulse"): Semos of Delos, *F. Gr. Hist.* 396 F. 34, ed. Jacoby.

22. In the inscriptions from Delos, the *phallos* is the "statue," the *agalma* of Dionysos: P. Bruneau, *Recherches sur les cultes de Délos* (Paris, 1970), pp. 314–317.

23. Aristotle, *Metaphysics,* Book V, 12, 1019 a 15, cited in English translation from Richard McKeon, ed., *The Basic Works of Aristotle* (New York: Random House, 1941). *Dunamis* is a personified power. Its cult appeared in Miletus and Teos and as *Automatia* in Syracuse and *Automatos* in Pergamon.

24. XXII–XXVII. Cf. I. M. Lonie, "On the Botanical Excursus in *De Natura Pueri* 22–27," *Hermes* 97 (1969): 391–411.

25. Seed of the living and succulence of the fruits: domain of *Liber* according to Varro (Augustine, *City of God,* VII, 21). One could make the notions employed in this botanical excursus correspond term by term with a series of epithets of a Dionysos "of nature."

26. *Scholia to Aristophanes, Acharnians,* 242 a, ed. N. G. Wilson, 1975, p. 42.

27. Indicated by H. Jeanmaire, *Dionysos,* pp. 27–28. The term is in Aischylos, *Persians* 614–615 for pure wine, born of the "savage mother." In Philoxenos of Leucas, F. 836 C, ed. Page (*Poetae Melici Graeci*).

28. For example, the Couretes in the hymn addressed to the

Couros: they leapt (*thore*), and they hailed the all-powerful master of the *ganos*.

29. Cf. M. Guarducci, "Bryaktes" (1962), reprinted in *Scritti scelti sulla religione greca e romana e sul cristianesimo* (Leyden, 1983), pp. 10–17.

30. Euripides, *Bacchae* 107, with a properly voluminous comment by J. Roux (*Euripide,* vol. 2, pp. 281–283).

31. Dionysos multiplying grapes (*Orphic Hymn* 53.10), as he is painted in Pompeii before Vesuvius, head crowned and grapes at his feet, pouring a libation.

32. *Bruein,* in Hesychios (s.v.) is glossed as *pedan.*

33. Timotheus, F. 780, ed. Page (*Poetae Melici Graeci*).

34. Verse cited in Stobaeus, *Eclogae Physicae* I, 2, 31 (according to Guarducci, "Bryaktes," p. 12): Pan the Dancer, the bounding goat. Silenus, *Palatine Anthology* 9.756.

INDEX

89

Index

Index